Build Your Dream

12 Essential Tools
For Successful Living

Byron E. Thompson

Build Your Dream: 12 Essential Tools for Successful Living

Published by Wheatmark®
610 East Delano Street, Suite 104
Tucson, Arizona 85705 U.S.A.
www.wheatmark.com

International Standard Book Number: 978-1-60494-280-4
Library of Congress Control Number: 2009930783

To Patricia

Contents

A Bag of Tools

Isn't it strange

That princes and kings,

And clowns that caper in sawdust rings,

And common people

Like you and me

Are builders of eternity?

Each is given a bag of tools,

A shapeless mass,

A book of rules,

And each must make

—Ere life is flown—

A stumbling block

Or a steppingstone.

R. L. Sharpe

A Life Worth Living

"I have imagined a life which should be that of the average man in average circumstances, and still grand, heroic."

—Walt Whitman

This is a book about you—your hopes, your dreams, and your desires, and how to make them come true. While I don't know you personally, I know some things about you because of the things we all have in common as human beings.

We all want to live rich, balanced, successful lives. Not just a financially secure life—that's the easy part—but also one that enables you to participate fully, effectively, and abundantly.

You're able to achieve such a life because you have two important resources available to you. First, your personal assets, in the form of nearly limitless, untapped, latent abilities, which, with proper training, can be developed to achieve any goal you set. Second, the unlimited opportunities available to you in a free society, which allows you to become all you can be.

Your Entitlement

You are entitled to such a life and it is possible for you to excel in your career in today's fast-paced, demanding world, while living the balanced, satisfying life you crave. You not only deserve to live your ideal life, you owe it to yourself.

And I'm going to show you how to get it.

What is the payoff? Why should you make the effort to create your ideal life? Is it worth it?

Benefits of Creating a Life Worth Living

1. You achieve a high standard of living, one that is consistent with your values.

2. You do the right work and experience the thrill of expressing your best self, using all of your talents.

3. You feel the satisfaction of making a significant contribution to the world; you know that your life matters.

4. You experience happiness, contentment, peace, and freedom from stress.

5. You live life more vividly, with a feeling of aliveness and enthusiasm.

Choosing the Essentials

What do you need to do to gain these benefits?

Adopt and practice the essential tools in this book for abundant, joyful living. They have been used by others to successfully pursue happiness. I've learned to identify and use these tools based on more than thirty-five years of experience in the human potential development field. I owned and operated a Dale Carnegie franchise, conducting in-depth training programs in the areas of developing human relations skills, attitude control, self-confidence, enthusiasm, and overcoming worry. During that time I have trained over twenty-five thousand success-minded men and women as they worked toward realizing their dreams.

Using Your Potential

How did I become so deeply involved in human potential development? A defining experience and a life-changing discovery started me on my journey.

When I was a young boy, two uncles who were psychology majors at Ohio State University repeatedly tested me. Although I don't recall a great deal about those tests, my selective memory told me that I had scored well on the Binet-Simon scale which tests for intelligence.

So I cherished the *belief* that I was intelligent, ignoring the poor grades that caused me to drop out of college in my freshman year until, at nineteen, I had an eye-opening conversation with one of those uncles. With all the arrogance that only a smart-aleck, know-it-all kid can have, I brushed off my lack of achievement, explaining to my uncle Bob that I was still going to do great things in life because I had a high I.Q. After all, he'd tested me and told me so. Bob patiently explained to me that I.Q. only measures *potential* capacity. In the same way that an eight-ounce glass has the potential to hold eight ounces of liquid, the I.Q. score merely tells you the quantity of knowledge you're capable of absorbing. It's just latent ability if you don't develop it. He said, "If you only put two ounces of liquid in your eight-ounce glass, you are no better off than a person who has a two-ounce glass but fills it to the top." It didn't take a lot of intelligence for me to get his point.

Bob's explanation helped me understand why I finished in that 10 percent of my high school graduating class that made the upper 90 percent possible.

After an undistinguished, mediocre stint in the military and a succession of dead-end jobs, I knew I needed to change something to get better results in my life. That's when I discovered the value of participating in self-improvement and personal development training programs. These were the kinds of programs my teachers never told me about in school. They were invaluable in helping me to understand how to develop my latent abilities. I participated in a wide variety of them— some good, some not so good—but I learned something from all of them. They gave me a new vision of my possibilities, increased my self-confidence, and provided me with the skills I was later able to use when I worked in Dale Carnegie. Here are the most important lessons I learned from those training programs, which you can use now:

- We're only using about ten percent of our total potential ability.
- There are fundamental tools for success in life that can be quickly developed to use more of that potential.
- Belief in ourselves is as important as our native intelligence.
- This confidence is a result of having a series of successful experiences and redefining ourselves in light of those successes.

Bag of Tools and Book of Rules

Throughout my career, I've read, traveled, observed, and trained people to be more successful. And as one who identifies with the poet, Walt Whitman's "average man in average circumstance," I share his vision of a "grand and heroic" life. Furthermore, I've learned from successful people how each of us can create such a life for ourselves.

This book contains the bag of tools and the book of rules necessary to achieve success as *you* define it. It is designed to help you rewrite the script of your life, to be a participant, architect, and builder of a life that is even more vivid and richly textured than perhaps you now enjoy. The payoff is a greater degree of satisfaction and control over the quality of your life than you ever imagined.

Who Should Read This Book?

This book is valuable for anyone who is serious about achieving more from life. It is especially appropriate for you if you are going through a passage. That's the term used by Gail Sheehy in her best-selling book, *Passages*, which defines our life crises, or transitions. Perhaps your passage is in the form of a change in relationship, career change, financial circumstances, or a change in attitude about yourself or your life. Wherever you are in your search for a life worth living, this book is for you.

This Book Can Help You

Many successful executives, professional athletes, and academics—men and women alike—have written books on success. They cause us to say to ourselves, " Wow! That's great, but I'm no (fill in the name of the last book on success you read, written by a famous person). I'm just an ordinary person." This, then, is a book for you and every other ordinary person, written by an ordinary man who found a way to make his dream come true and documented the process as he went along.

If your life from now on gives you one-tenth the joy and satisfaction mine has given me, it will be well worth the read.

Quotations

You'll note that I've used quotations to illustrate major points, some from famous people, some from people who are not so well known. These thoughts are often the result of years of contemplation. Let's not regard these quotes lightly, but respect them and use them as guideposts on our journey.

I've also used examples from my own life to illustrate the points I want to make—but the book is not about me. Please don't take my word for the effectiveness of the techniques I'm suggesting here. They have worked for many of my clients and produced great results; your results may be even better. I only ask you to keep an open mind and try the ideas I suggest. If they make sense to you, adopt them and adapt them to your unique situation. If they don't, throw them out.

A Note about Humor

I've made liberal use of humorous stories to illustrate important points throughout the book. These stories all make a point and will provide you with a momentary mental shift as we deal with the serious discussion of your life.

Before you begin—a reminder: Use caution when listening to others; you are the only one who can decide what actions are best for you.

Humor: Two motorists collide at an intersection. Their cars were damaged but no one was hurt. Surveying the damage, John pulls out a flask and says, "You look pretty shook up. Let's have a drink to settle our nerves."

Bill sighs, "Thanks." He takes a big drink of the whiskey and hands it back to John, who puts it back in his pocket.

"Aren't you going to have a drink?" asks Bill.

"No!" exclaims John, " Not yet. I'll wait 'til after the police get here and finish their report."

Even though this book contains the best I've got, you still might want to ask, "What's best for me?" before taking advice from me or anyone else.

Good luck! Lets have fun and create a life worth living.

Suggestions for Getting the Most from This Book!

Read this book thoughtfully; that is, take time to think between chapters. I suggest you read one chapter a day the first time through, for a fast start, then read it a second time; one chapter a week. Taking more time to think will allow you to go into greater detail and depth in each area. The majority of the benefit you'll derive from this book will come from your own thinking and doing.

To assist you in organizing your thoughts and integrating the concepts into your own plan for success, I've included a question and answer exercise at the end of each chapter. Record your answers in order to capture your frame of mind at that moment.

Review your answers each week as you progress through the book, since each chapter builds on the previous one. Modify your answers, making additions and amendments as you create your ideal life. These modifications are healthy signs of growth. This is the path to increasing our belief in ourselves—we grow through our successes. Our self-image becomes more positive and our self-confidence increases.

Find someone to whom you can hold yourself accountable: a mentor, spouse, partner, co-worker or buddy. If you're able to find someone who is doing these exercises at the same time, you can support and help one another. Promise that you will report your progress to that other person on a pre-set schedule. The commitment to being accountable to another person and to a deadline will force you to function in a way that leaving it open-ended will not. "What we all most need is someone to make us do what we know we ought to do." Ralph Waldo Emerson

Take one action step, however small, to implement a key idea that will improve the quality of your life.

Part One

Foundations for Success

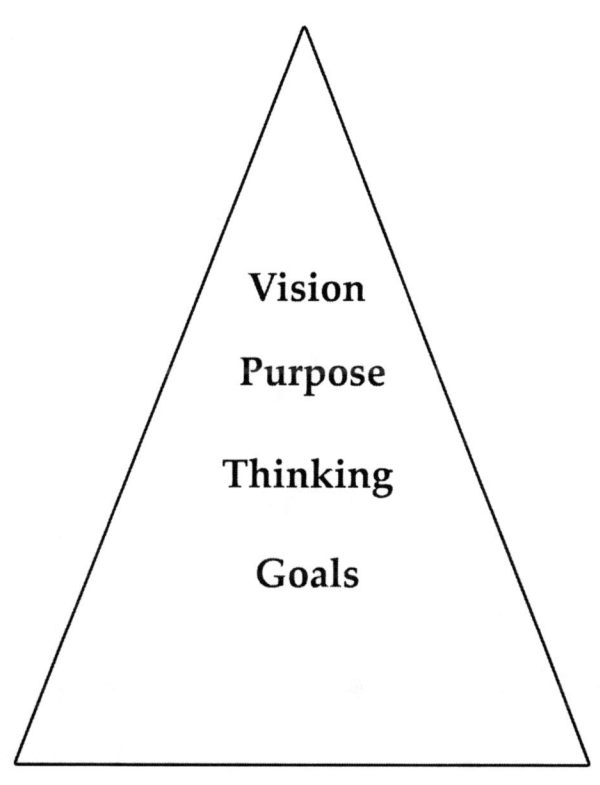

Vision

Purpose

Thinking

Goals

The First Essential Tool

Vision

"Vision is the art of seeing things invisible."
— Jonathan Swift

The Most Important Decision of Your Life

I had a decision to make. The bridge was as high as a fifteen-story building. I stood on the platform looking down at the water, ankles strapped together, getting ready to dive — *if I had the nerve to do it!*

It was to be my first-ever bungy jump and I was terrified. As I looked down into that chasm, my heart pounded and adrenalin surged through me.

My wife and I were celebrating our wedding anniversary with a trip to Australia and New Zealand. On New Zealand's South Island, near Queenstown, we came to the Kawarau Bridge, site of the first bungy jump. On an impulse, we decided to try it.

I shuffled out to the edge of the platform and with the reassurance of my coach was preparing to jump, when an overwhelming wave of fear swept over me. I looked over at the viewing platform to the crowd gathering there, young and old. I realized that each of them also had the opportunity to jump, and probably, after a careful one-second consideration, had prudently declined.

I considered my options. I could bail out, not an uncommon choice I was told, and make up a story for the spectators. Or I could face my fear and jump. If successful, I would gain all the rewards that accompany any choice in life that requires us to draw on our courage: self-confidence, decisiveness, personal power, etc.

As I stood there trying to decide, my mind raced back through the years and I thought about fear, my old enemy. Fear always seems to exert itself whenever I'm on the verge of attempting anything I think is risky: Fear of failure. Fear of embarrassment. Fear of looking bad. Fear of performing poorly. Fear of others laughing at me.

Like so many times before, I desperately wanted to bail out. It didn't matter what the choice was—choosing to have a family, leaving a secure, salaried career to work on commission, or a life choice of any kind that could reward me with the life I'd always dreamed of living—my old enemy fear would be there.

Life is a lot like a bungy jump.

We can either experience the sense of aliveness and the excitement of participating fully in life, or we can stand back and observe. You undoubtedly know this from the courageous choices you've already made in your own life.

So you'll understand the thoughts that were racing through my mind, as I stood paralyzed, realizing that it was more than a decision about a bungy jump.

> "The safest place for a ship is in the harbor. But that's not what ships are built for!"
>
> —Grace Murray Hopper

It was a choice of either living fully or giving in to my fear. I looked down at the river below and decided that *living is more important*.

I looked out at the horizon as my coach instructed me, took a deep breath and … dove off headfirst.

The wind whistled in my ears and I could feel the coolness of the air as I plunged toward the river below. At the last second I felt the elastic band grab hold and propel me back up toward the bridge. As I bounced up and down I yelled, *"YESSS!"*

While I stopped bouncing and waited to be lowered into the boat below, my mind whirled, "What a thrill! What a sensation of being alive! What a sense of achievement! What an exciting experience!"

It's a memory I'll carry with me the rest of my life! My courageous wife Patricia was the next to jump and as we climbed the stairs to the viewing platform chattering exuberantly to each other, it was clear that it had been equally thrilling for her. When we reached the top of the stairs, the excited spectators crowded around us, "What was it like?" "Were you scared?" "Did it hurt?" "Would you do it again?" Several said, "I could never do that."

Because you chose to read this book, I suspect you are ready for a bungy jump experience of another kind; an experience that includes your aspirations for a richer, more rewarding, and satisfying life. Good News! You don't have to risk your life to experience that sense of vitality and accomplishment.

"Well," you might say, "maybe I do and maybe I don't aspire to all that stuff. I don't know." Here's a sure way to find out. Just answer this question: *If they were to make a movie of your life, would you pay to see it?* (Never mind who plays the part of you in the movie.) The question really is: Is your life as dramatic, fun, interesting, and rewarding as you would like it to be?

You are at this very moment standing on a precipice overlooking the rest of your life, and you have a choice to make. It is the most important choice of your life. It is not a matter of life or death, but one of choosing ongoing aliveness. Make each new day an adventure! Escape from boredom and blandness. "Most men lead lives of quiet desperation and go to the grave with the song still in them," said Henry David Thoreau. You can either play it safe by opting for a life of predictable monotony, or you can go for it and achieve an exhilarating, memorable life worth living.

Let's get started, then.

Creating a Successful Life

There are twelve essential tools for creating an extraordinary life, which I'll give to you one at a time. The discussion and examples around each tool are designed to condition you for the action portion of the book. That vital portion comes in the form of questions and suggested actions at the end of each chapter.

My work and studies have enabled me to achieve a level of success and happiness that is far beyond any I thought possible. My accomplishments might be modest compared to yours or to the ones to which you aspire, but I've achieved them as an average man in average circumstances. That is the most encouraging piece of information I have to offer you. If *I* was able to do it, you can do it.

Knuckle-baller Phil Neikro, one of about twenty pitchers in the history of major league baseball to record over three hundred career wins, said, "If I had to give young pitchers today advice on how to get three hundred wins, I'd tell them—literally—to take it one pitch at a time. They should use me as a model. Only a handful of guys can throw a ball as hard as Nolan Ryan or Roger Clemens but with the kind of junk I threw, if I can win three hundred games, anyone can."

It's time now to get into action and take the first step on your adventure by answering some questions.

First Essential Tool: Vision

Questions and Actions

This is an exercise in imagination; draw upon your creativity. This is not planning or goal-setting. You aren't committing to taking any action at this point. Sit quietly and think about the questions. There are no wrong answers. This is an exercise in possibility thinking. Before you start remind yourself of the inspiring words of Helen Keller:

"Life is either a daring adventure or nothing. Security does not exist in nature, nor do the children of men as a whole experience it. Avoiding danger is no safer in the long run than exposure."

1. What will your life look like in all areas in the next five years if there are no limits on your success or your growth potential?

2. Ideally, where will you be living? Which country? What part of it?

3. What kind of personal relationship will you be in, if everything is perfect?

4. What kind of work will you be doing? Not necessarily a new career or job, but an improvement in the quality of the work you're doing now.

5. How will your health and fitness be? How will it have improved?

6. What kind of social life will you have? Is it more active and interesting? For example, do you have a larger network of friends? Are you involved in a new sport or hobby? Are you taking classes?

7. What will your spiritual life be like?

8. What sort of community involvement will you have? What groups will you belong to?

9. Are there any other ideal conditions and/or circumstances you'd like to have in your life? If so, describe them. Note: The sky's the limit here. Be creative! We're planning an ideal destination for our journey for now. It will probably change as we go along. It will probably get better.

10. What single step will you take today to make your vision a reality?

"The idea is to seek a vision that gives you purpose in life and then to implement that vision. The vision by itself is one half—one part—of a process. It implies the necessity of living that vision; otherwise the vision will sink back into itself."

—Lewis P. Johnson

The Second Essential Tool

Purpose

"This is the true joy in life, the being used for a purpose recognized by yourself as a mighty one."

—George Bernard Shaw

The Vital Question

I herded my wife and two daughters off the plane in front of me, frightened, yet filled with anticipation. We'd just landed at JFK after a long, tiring flight from Madrid this hot June day. It was good to walk on American soil again, after living in a small village in Mallorca, Spain, for the past eighteen months.

We claimed our beat-up luggage and went through customs, drawing suspicious looks from the agent, since we looked a little disreputable. My scraggly two-year-old beard needed to be trimmed as much as my long hair, and my wife's tie-dyed, hippie-style dress was enough to make us suspect. We were saved from delay by the enthusiasm of our eight- and ten-year old angelic-looking daughters.

Our ultimate destination, three thousand miles away, was Chico, California, a small town that had been our home before we'd chucked it all to start a new life in Spain. Our plan hadn't worked out because I'd underestimated the difficulty of adapting to a new country, culture, and language. My savings evaporated twice as fast as I'd expected, and so we were heading home— disappointed and discouraged.

The experience hadn't been totally negative. We never missed a meal or went without a safe place to live, and we met a lot of interesting people. We'd expanded our view of the world as only living abroad can do. But now we were back, face to face with reality, taking inventory of our resources. We had one fifty-dollar traveler's check and a handful of loose bills. Things didn't look too promising.

We were funneled into a taxi and gave the driver the Manhattan address of my friend, Bob James. Bob and I had worked together in the Dale Carnegie business and been close friends for ten years in California before he and his wife Betty moved to New York. I'd called him from Barcelona a few weeks earlier to tell him we were on our way home and would be passing through New York. Even though he hadn't heard from me in over a year, he said I was welcome to bring Patricia and the girls to stay with him and his wife for a few days.

I stared out the window as we rode into Manhattan, thinking about the immensity of the mess I'd gotten us into.

It all started three years before. I was sitting in a meeting in Scottsdale, Arizona. I was thirty-five years old, plugging away at a corporate sales job at the Magnavox Company, raising a family, paying bills, saving for retirement, but not really satisfied. A speaker that morning talked about our retirement plan, which was a good one, but all I could see ahead of me was thirty more years of plodding—working—saving. It didn't sound exciting.

The next speaker was Dr. Eugene Jennings, a professor from Michigan State University. Referring to the previous presentation, Dr. Jennings said, "That was interesting. I'm interested in retirement. I'm interested in the numbers of men and women who have already retired but haven't given their companies the courtesy of notifying them. They are still drawing a salary, but they are sitting on their hands, not giving their companies the best that they've got." He went on to say, "I've done a lot of work in the field of geriatrics, working with older people. I can tell you that there is nothing sadder for a person, upon reaching the age of retirement, than to look in the mirror and realize that, in an ultimate sense, they'd settled for less than their best."

At that moment, I made the decision to *not* allow that to happen to me. I didn't know what I wanted at that point; I only knew what I didn't want. I didn't want a life of mediocrity, full of regrets. Jennings' closing question rang in my ears for weeks after I left Scottsdale. In wrapping up his presentation, he said, "You only live once, but if you do it right, once is enough."

That is how, after much soul searching and many long, late-evening conversations with my wife, we found ourselves a year later in Barcelona, Spain. We came in search of a life of adventure— in search of a life that would be memorable, rich, and vivid. We wanted lives that were meaningful and interesting.

But that idealized fantasy wasn't to be. It seemed that after a series of disappointments and setbacks, our dream was shattered. It wasn't until much later, when we were able to put the entire experience in perspective, that we realized it was probably the smartest decision of our lives.

I'd always considered myself to be a resourceful person. But that wasn't the case in Spain, as I tried to accomplish the most rudimentary aspects of day-to-day living. We had little time left for the life-enriching experiences we were hoping for before we left our secure environment in California.

The only bright spot on the horizon was the upcoming visit with my loving, understanding, accepting friend, Bob James. Surely he'd have words of solace, some sage advice and hopefully some money to get me out of the mess I'd gotten myself into. Arriving at Bob and Betty's apartment, we rang the bell and the James' welcomed us with hugs and warm greetings. After a delicious meal and a good night's sleep, we spent the next day catching up. Betty was a ticket sales supervisor for American Airlines, and Bob had moved to

Manhattan to take a position with the Dale Carnegie organization, a training company. He had always been a serious student of psychology and religion and later published a couple of very thought-provoking books, *Journey of a Soul* and *Discovering Your Best Self.* Things were going well for Bob and Betty, and they looked healthy and prosperous.

"How's it going for you, Byron?" he asked.

Trying to hold my emotions in check, I blurted out the whole story. "To be honest, Bob, not so good. Living in Spain was a lot more expensive and difficult than I ever anticipated. I'm three thousand miles from home. I'm dead broke, since we sold our house to finance our adventure. I don't have a job, and the prospects of getting one don't look too good; the country is in a serious recession and my resume won't look very good with a two-year gap. I think I made a big mistake. I feel like a total loser."

He nodded and gazed at me with a penetrating stare. Then he asked the most disturbing question anyone had ever asked me. "What business are you in, Byron?"

I couldn't believe my ears! I'd just poured my heart out to him, and he'd reacted as though he hadn't heard me at all! "Weren't you listening?" I exploded. "I don't have a business, I don't have a job, I don't have any money, and I don't have any idea how I'm going to get my family back to California!"

He smiled and said, "Oh, I heard you perfectly. I'm not worried about you. You'll be all right. My question really is," he paused until he had my complete attention, "*What business are you in as a man?*

"You see," he went on, looking at me kindly, "I know your whole life has been a journey to find yourself, to find that thing you were uniquely created to do. To identify that singular thing, you have to answer the most important question any person has to answer. Why are you here? What's your purpose in life? What business are you in as a person?"

Bob's question stunned me. I couldn't answer him on the spot. "What business am I in? What business am I in?"

As we got settled in California, I thought of that question day and night. We found a temporary place to live and both Patricia and I found temporary jobs to make ends meet.

Your Inspirational Answer

All the while the question kept nagging at me. What business am I in? What is my ultimate purpose in life? What is my destiny? After asking myself the question over and over, I realized the answer. It gave me what I'd been searching for the previous twenty years.

I was excited! I immediately called Bob and shouted into the phone, "I've got it! The 'what business am I in?' question! I've got the answer."

He said, "Oh yes. What did you come up with?"

I said, "I'm in the business of helping other people to grow."

"What do you mean?"

I explained, "That's my purpose in life, that's what I do. It doesn't matter whether I'm sitting down with a friend, on my feet speaking to a group, or conducting a training program. All I want to do is to help people. It doesn't even seem to matter whether or not I get paid."

"That's it!" Bob said excitedly into the phone. "Tell me more!"

To illustrate what I meant, I told him a story. Just a few months before, while in Barcelona, I took Patricia to the finals of a national classical guitar competition. There were two or three hundred people in attendance, many dressed elegantly in tuxedos and gowns. A panel of judges sat in the front row of the first balcony just above us. The program began and the first four of five finalists came out in turn, looking very serious. They sat down and played flaw-lessly—or so it seemed to my untrained ear. Each of those first four contestants was identical: Young men in tuxedos. New, expensive-looking, inlaid, classical guitars. Each one played a superb classical selection. When they finished, they stood and bowed formally to the judges and the audience amid polite applause.

Then the final contestant came out. She was a slim young woman wearing a soft, light blue gown. Her long hair was pinned up in a loose bun, held with a Spanish comb. Her guitar was obviously old but well tended and polished. She looked up at the judges and smiled, then at the audience. As she sat down and began to play, I could feel the hair standing up on the back of my neck. She played flawless classical guitar at a level beyond anything else we'd heard that evening. The shadings and tonal nuances were obvious, even to an untrained listener. She was oblivious to the audience and the judges. She was totally engrossed in her music, creating magic with her fingers on that old guitar. She exuded peacefulness and contentment with that beautiful smile, which she wore during the entire performance.

When she finished, that very proper Catalan audience came to their feet, applauding and cheering as though they were at a rock concert. Well, there was no question about who had won; the judges called her back after a very short deliberation and presented her with her certificate and check. As Patricia and I walked in silence back to our *pension*, we still felt the enchantment of her music. After a while I turned to Patricia and said, "You know what my fantasy is? I imagine the first four contestants going home and, surrounded by friends and family, have a glass of wine, talk about the competition, why they didn't win, and what they need to do next year in order to win. But I see a different scene for her. I see her going back to her room alone, maybe in the *Barrio Gotico*, pouring herself a little *copa* of sherry. She looks at the check, smiles, and casually tosses it, along with the first place certificate, on the table. She lets her hair down and takes off her shoes, picks up her guitar and starts to play."

I was more than a little emotional as I relived that thrilling evening. "You see, Bob, she wasn't playing for first prize or the money or the judges vote or the audience's approval. She was playing because that's who she *is*. She was using her highest and best talents. I believe she was doing the one thing she was uniquely created to do.

"She absolutely inspired me. I didn't realize at the time that she was modeling my future for me. I want that quality of being for myself. I want to help other people grow because that's who I am as a person. I think that's the thing I am destined to do. Do you see what I mean?"

Now he was excited too. "As long as that's so, you might as well earn your living doing it. That way you'll have more time to dedicate to it and you'll have to become an expert. You'll have to produce measurable results for people so you can justify getting paid for helping them grow."

The Vital Action

That made sense to me. I knew the best place for me to work was in the Dale Carnegie business, helping people use their highest and best skills, encouraging people's growth, and getting paid for it. There were just two small problems. First, I had been a failure in Dale Carnegie work before. The nature of the business required selling, and I wasn't a good enough salesman to sell at the required professional level. The second problem was the owner of the company where I wanted to work. Boo Bue, a practical businessman, knew that I couldn't sell. I doubted that he would take another chance on me, but my desire to succeed was so strong that I prepared a sales presentation focused on why he should hire me. I called him for an appointment. He agreed to see me, and as I went to meet him, my heart raced. What if he turned me down? I didn't have a back-up plan. This was it!

We sat down in his office and I blurted out the reasons he had to hire me. Number one, he didn't have a salesperson in the territory where I lived, so he wasn't getting any business from there anyway. Number two, I was dead broke and desperate, so I'd have to work hard or my family wouldn't be able to eat. To this day I don't know what motivated Boo to take a chance on me, but he did. He said, "Okay Byron, we'll try it, but I want you to know there's no salary; it is straight commission, you'll only get paid for what you sell and you'll have to send me weekly reports." It was the beginning of a mutually beneficial partnership. He became my mentor and champion, and our partnership matured into a friendship that endures to this day.

The next five years were the most exciting, challenging, and fulfilling years of my life. Psychologist Abraham Maslow, author of *Toward a Psychology of Being,* coined the term "peak experience," a condition that exists when one is so wrapped up in an experience that he or she loses track of time and space and is on an emotional high. That was me. I set a goal, with the help of my wife, to own my own franchise training company. The appointment would depend on availability, which was scarce, and competition, which was stiff. Fortunately, Boo agreed to help me achieve my goal if I did everything he asked me to do. I did so, and worked with a dedication and passion I'd never felt before. I had a definite major purpose—to borrow a term used by Napoleon Hill in his book, *Think and Grow Rich*—and a major goal. I was exhilarated and alive, more creative and happy than I'd ever been.

I look back now and realize that it was a fortunate confluence of events and circumstances that led to the discovery of my purpose in life and my ability to identify and set a major goal. The insights I gained from that experience are the reasons I've been able to achieve the success I have, and why I'm uniquely qualified to help others to realize their dreams.

I had an advantage that most people never get in their lifetimes. I started with a clean slate. I had no money, no job, no credentials, and no track record to speak of. I started over from scratch. I was able to spend a lot of time thinking, distilling, analyzing, and recording in my journal the lessons I learned from my teaching and my life experiences.

So When Bob James asked me that life-defining question, I was already preconditioned to answer it and thereby alter the course of my life. If I had stayed with Magnavox, or with any company where I had a logical career path in front of me, I would not have been able to see the unlimited opportunities available to me.

This book is an opportunity for you to benefit from my mistakes and the resulting lessons I learned.

Purpose in Life

Obviously, not everyone has the same career goals. However, as I discovered in my work of helping others achieve success, the steps to attaining goals are the same. I had to overcome long odds to achieve my goal and was required to draw upon resources deep within myself—resources I'd only suspected were there. Most importantly, I found the discovery of a major purpose to be necessary to realizing my dream.

History tells us that all great achievements, accompanied by satisfaction and happiness, are triumphs of purpose. Winston Churchill's focus enabled England to prevail against the tyranny of Adolph Hitler. Mahatma Gandhi's vision of a free India is an inspiration to all freedom-loving people. Mother Teresa's dedication to serving people could only come from the embrace of a higher purpose. She loved her work, accepted no payment, and was so highly revered that she was beatified shortly after her death. We may not possess the talent and intelligence of these leaders or have challenges as great as theirs, but the philosophy and mechanics for achieving fulfillment, satisfaction, and success in life are the same.

Every one of us has, at heart, a fundamental passion—whether we have identified it or not—that subconsciously affects every aspect of our lives. Being in sync with that passion creates drive and satisfaction not available through other means.

There is no more important task for us than to undertake the rewarding journey of discovering and surrendering to our purpose. It is my fervent hope that this book will help you by asking questions that will identify or clarify your purpose in life and give you the tools to make your dream a reality.

My purpose remains unchanged. It is to help the maximum number of people to realize their full potential, and it is uniquely mine. Your purpose, too, must be uniquely yours. Our purposes must come from within, not predetermined by the media, our parents, or our teachers. That is not to say we should reject everything we've learned; rather, we must go deep within ourselves and listen to the inner voice, which guides us. That voice will separate other's opinions from what is really true for us.

My experience has taught me that whatever stage of life you are in, you have within you a dream waiting to be uncovered, a big, exciting—even noble—vision. It may not be fully formed in your mind, but the potential is there, waiting to surface. Let's start by asking, *"What business are you in?"*

You may not be able to answer this immediately. When you do, you'll have a mission. One that is strong enough to defeat the incessant nagging of that inner voice of self-doubt that inevitably arises when one takes on a really big challenge.

Luckily, as we achieve goal after goal and our basic needs are satisfied, new goals surface as the next logical expression of our purpose.

Once our definite major purpose or mission becomes clear, it can serve as a roadmap for decision-making. It will serve as a moral compass so we won't kid ourselves about what is right and what is wrong for us. It enables us to be true to ourselves. As Shakespeare said in *Hamlet*, "This above all: to thine own self be true. And it must follow, as the night the day, thou canst not be false to any man."

Boo Bue, my mentor, is an example of this integrity. He always carried a photograph of his children with him because he valued being an outstanding father. He told me that whenever he had an ethical decision to make, he'd ask himself, "Would this decision make Brian and Karen proud?" The point here is that successful people typically are driven by meaningful, rather than superficial, values.

Humor: A yuppie got out of his new Porsche on a busy Los Angeles street just as a truck sped by and ripped off the door. The distraught car owner stood there, repeating over and over, "My car! My car!"

A police cruiser pulled up, and as the officer approached him, the yuppie said, "Look at my car! It's ruined!" The incredulous police officer replied, "Never mind your car, your arm is missing!" "Oh no!" said the yuppie. "My Rolex is gone!"

Values and Balance

Our purpose must be tied to deeper values that contribute in some way to making this world a better place to live. Following a dream with great passion can end in disappointment, even when it seems that one has been successful, if that goal is not built on a solid foundation of values.

American literature is filled with examples of goal attainment without ethics. F. Scott Fitzgerald's commentary on this condition in America in *The Great Gatsby* is a classic. Sloan Wilson brought us *The Man in the Gray Flannel Suit,* in which his money-driven protagonist trades honesty for hypocrisy. Rabbi Harold Kushner, in *When Everything You've Ever Wanted Is Not Enough,* reports counseling people on their deathbeds. Those who had the most difficulty accepting death were those who realized that their lives hadn't ultimately mattered, that they hadn't contributed anything to the world. On the other hand, those people who accepted death most graciously believed their living had made a difference.

So I wanted to make a difference and be successful, but not at the expense of those things that really mattered to me. I *did* want to make enough money for my family and me to be comfortable and to be charitable to others. The Bible is often misquoted as, "money is the root of all evil," rather than, "the *love* of money is the root of all evil."

The person who doesn't know when he has enough will never have enough. All of these thoughts, with respect to values and the role money plays in one's happiness, demand that we embrace the advice of Socrates to, "know thyself."

I realized that no matter how much talent or education I might have, I wouldn't be able to achieve anything significant in my life until I had a purpose, a reason greater than just earning a living to pay my bills. I wouldn't be able to attain the success and balanced quality of life I so desperately wanted. And so, in that post-Spain period, I began an exciting journey; one that continues to this day.

Before a person can find ultimate contentment, he or she must first find a burning passion to do something important. Their destiny or passion may never be consciously articulated; nonetheless it is there, allowing them to express their highest and best selves. We've all known happy, contented people like this in all kinds of jobs, using their natural talents to do their work with excellence. At best, failure to manifest this passion can create a frustrating life of discontent. At worst, it may cause a dispirited, depressing attitude of compromise and mediocrity. The resulting inner anxiety, when unacknowledged, can manifest itself in a wide variety of psychosomatic, life-limiting, physical ailments, according to psychologist

Rollo May in *The Meaning of Anxiety.* It creates a life of compromise and substitution for the real thing.

Our passion, on the other hand, provides the ongoing inspiration to set and achieve worthwhile goals and to overcome setbacks and discouragement.

I've talked to architects, bankers, doctors, lawyers, engineers, and business people, who are absolutely crazy about what they do; for them, their work was more than a job or a profession. They felt as though they had been called to do their special work, even to make a contribution to the quality of life in the world. In pursuing their passion, they developed a harmonious relationship with themselves. Their lives were filled with joy, satisfaction, completion and abundance on a regular basis.

What is Success?

Most certainly this group's definition of success more closely conforms to Ralph Waldo Emerson's definition:

"To laugh often and love much; to win the respect of intelligent persons and the affection of children; to earn the approbation of honest critics and to endure the betrayal of false friends; to appreciate beauty; to find the best in others; to give oneself; to leave the world a bit better, whether by a healthy child, a garden patch or a redeemed social condition; to have played and laughed with enthusiasm and sung with exultation; to know even one life has breathed easier because you have lived: this is to have succeeded."

Financial Success and Balance

In spite of an inclination to embrace Emerson's broader, more balanced values, it shouldn't come as a surprise that the majority of these successful people also did well financially. They are not necessarily the high profile, super-rich we read about in Forbes and Fortune magazines. Rather, they frequently fit the profile of those millionaires featured in Thomas Stanley and William Danko's extensively researched book, *The Millionaire Next Door*. The character-istics of those millionaires profiled in the authors' in-depth research were:

- Frugality—They are not conspicuous consumers. They do not live in big houses—indeed they tend to live in middle-class neighborhoods—nor do they drive flashy cars. You will not see them in Armani suits.

- Prudence—They tend to allocate their funds efficiently, in-vesting in ways to build wealth.

- Right livelihood—They chose their occupations based on sat-isfaction and potential to produce profitable results, rather than for prestige. They also credited their partner in life as a major contributor to their success.

- Conservative—They don't make an ostentatious display of success, preferring instead to enjoy the satisfaction that comes from their chosen way of life. They are typically active in their communities and their churches.

- There does not need to be a conflict between prosperity, en-joying abundance in one's life, and leading a worthwhile, valuable life.

You must define success in your own terms whether it is a ca-reer, a level of financial success, a relationship with specific char-acteristics, a spiritual condition, a community or political office. When it has been defined and you determine it to be worth your total commitment, nothing can prevent you from becoming the person you aspire to be!

Second Essential Tool: Purpose

Questions and Actions

What business are you in?

Remember, the answer does not necessarily relate to your work or career. It is another way of asking yourself, " Who am I, really? What do I stand for? What is my purpose in life?"

Don't be concerned if the answer doesn't come to you right away. We'll do a number of exercises that will help you find the answer to that question.

Thinking

"Until thought is linked with purpose, there is no intelligent accomplishment."

—James Allen

"What business are you in?" A tough question. Where do we go to find the answer? What tools are available?

Wise men have been in disagreement over many things in the six thousand years of recorded history. On one thing they have unanimously agreed—our thoughts shape our lives. That is, we become what we think about all day long. That seems self-evident, but while the concept is not new, we don't always comprehend its significance.

The Bible says, "As a man thinketh, so in his heart is he." By thinking, we pursue the answer to that vital question. Once you have the answer to the question, "what business am I in?" you'll find, as I did, a dramatic shift in your thinking. If you are saying to yourself, "Wait, I don't know what my purpose is yet!" Don't worry, you will. How? By being convinced that until and unless you do get the answer to that question, you'll not achieve the life worth living we are after on this journey.

It's good to remind ourselves here of the inspiring words of Professor William James, the brilliant psychologist and philosopher who taught at Harvard University. These words of Dr. James meant so much to me—gave me hope and helped me fight discouragement as I undertook my journey: "Let no youth have any anxiety about the upshot of his education, whatever the line of it may be. For if he keeps faithfully busy each hour of the working day he can leave the final result to itself, for he'll wake up some fine morning and find himself one of the competent ones of his generation."

This discussion will help to stimulate your thought in pursuit of your purpose. The most powerful tool available to us is our ability to think. Our minds are a problem-solving, solution-finding tool. In order to do this, we need to program our subconscious mind in the same way we might program a computer. Since we become what we think about, we must take control of our thoughts. How?

One valuable method of directing our thought is to access the experiences and ideas others have chronicled by reading every book we can find on achieving success in our area of interest. We may re-read favorite books with renewed purpose and understanding. When we finally discover and are able to articulate our purpose, we will recognize that it has always been our purpose. It was there to discover at any time in our development. Mozart discovered it early, composing music at age four. Anna Mary Robertson, the painter better known as Grandma Moses, began to create her wonderful paintings in her mid-seventies. She painted until her death at age 101. Wherever you are, whether you've already specifically identified your purpose or are still searching, you are not wasting your time.

However, I would caution you not to let this realization be construed as permission to procrastinate or permit the "someday" syndrome to set in. Even the youngest of us is operating on a finite time schedule. John Lennon said, "Life is what happens while you are busy making other plans." We have a limited amount of time and it's not for any of us to know how long that is.

Sometimes it takes a dramatic life experience to become aware of the urgency to act. Michael Dalton was jolted into realizing this urgency as he drove his wife and newborn daughter home from the hospital. He said, "I looked in the rear view mirror and for the first time saw the baby in the car seat. I realized then that I had truly become an adult, with all the responsibilities that go with adulthood. I have a wife, a child, I'm a homeowner, and I'm thirty years old. I can't put off growing up any longer. I have to set about achieving my potential. I remember hearing song lyrics that said, "don't waste your time or time will waste you."

If we do not pursue a worthy ideal, then we must face the alternative—the loss of vitality and that nagging feeling that we've settled for less than the best life has to offer. We join that vast majority of people who lead empty, unfulfilled lives.

It is never too early to recognize our purpose in life and begin fulfilling it. Think of the tremendous business empire Paul Allen and Bill Gates created, founding Microsoft while still in their twenties!

Finding the Answer to the Question

At this point, if you are bogged down and wrestling with trying to answer the ultimate question of your destiny, I would suggest you start with any of the twelve tools in this book, whether goal-setting, writing and using affirmations, or any of the others. The twelve tools are an organic, rather than a linear, process. They all inter-connect and support the final goal of creating a life worth living. As you apply each of these tools, you'll move closer and closer to getting the answer to the question.

In other words, act as though you already know what your purpose is; you'll soon discover that it will all fit together when the answer comes.

In my own case, prior to the point in my life when my purpose became clear, everything I'd done, read and studied contributed to that defining point. Even though I didn't realize it at the time, all my activities made the recognition and fulfillment of my destiny inevitable. It was as though an inner, guiding force directed me.

Learning to Think

I re-read books such as *Think and Grow Rich* by Napoleon Hill, in which I first discovered of the concept of a definite major purpose in life as a focal point of one's thoughts. I also re-read James Allen's essay, *As a Man Thinketh*, in which he likened the human mind to a garden which produces good circumstances from good thoughts. As he explained it, these good thoughts can be planted like flowers, and weeding out bad thoughts can change undesirable circumstances. I listened again to Earl Nightingale's classic recording, *The Strangest Secret*, in which he quoted Dr. Albert Schweitzer's answer to the question, "What's wrong with men today?" Dr. Schweitzer answered, "Men simply don't think."

One of the most common complaints I heard from career-oriented people was how stressed they felt and how little time they had for themselves. With the advent of e-mail, instant messaging, PDAs, Twitter, the ubiquitous cell phone with its ever-expanding capabilities, and emphasis on multitasking, thinking gets squeezed out.

Lack of thinking time was certainly true in my own case. It seemed that I was always rushing to an imagined emergency or important appointment or event and there was never any time to just sit and think. I didn't value it as worthwhile activity.

Making Time to Think

I vividly recall learning a valuable lesson from Bob James, my friend in New York. He was sitting in a chair with his feet propped up on the coffee table, his hands behind his head and his eyes closed. Now, Bob has always impressed me with his ability to think in depth on complex subjects. He demonstrated this quality in his books and speeches, and when he achieved a Ph.D. in Theology. He made taking time to think a priority, and it paid big dividends for him.

I, like many people, hurried around doing something, anything, just to be moving. Bob didn't move until he knew what he was doing and why he was doing it.

By slowing down and thinking in a more deliberate, conscious way, I was able to achieve the things I value most. It was one of the most important habits I ever developed.

Defining Success

Earl Nightingale's definition of success is, "the progressive realization of a worthwhile goal or ideal." We'll talk more about progressively realizing our goals later, but for now, the key word is "worthwhile." Only you can define a worthwhile goal and that goal, I'll bet, is closely related to your purpose, giving you uncommon focus and vision. Wayne Gretzky, arguably the greatest hockey player in the National Hockey League, possessed this vision. When asked the secret of his success, The Great One replied, "I envision where the puck is going to be—and go there." Gretzky possessed an uncommon ability to instantaneously paint a picture in his mind of the successful outcome he wanted and the next step he needed to take to achieve it.

This same ability is the reason successful people in all fields—from Olympic gold medalists to top executives, and award winners of every kind—are frequently described as being single-minded or even obsessed. But I was interested in more than being obsessed with a single goal. I was intrigued with the idea that it might be possible to succeed in one's chosen field and to still live life fully, to experience it vividly. I looked for examples in my reading and study and looked for models in the people I met.

Psychology's Contribution

Psychological studies on healthy people contribute much to our understanding of success. The greatest contributors in this area were the humanists, most notably Dr. Abraham Maslow. His hierarchy of needs, with self-actualization at the top, provided tremendous insight into the feeling of satisfaction that comes from goal-attainment. His research demonstrated that as human beings we are driven by a progressive set of needs. Each need must be satisfied before we move on to the next. As an example, our own stomachs must be full before we think about donating to a charity. Maslow said we're motivated by survival at the most primary level, then the need for security, followed by the need to belong to a community, then a need for recognition, to feel as though we are important. The highest need he called self-actualization. We experience this state when we are at our best, contributing to the world, making a difference. This feeling of doing worthwhile work is a manifestation of an individual's attunement with his or her purpose. Maslow's theory also provides us with tremendous insights, not only into the satisfaction that accompanies goal attainment, but also the enigmatic nature of success when constructive discontent sets in.

Constructive discontent is a function of the growth of human beings, best described by Simone de Beauvoir, the French existentialist and author of *The Second Sex*, like this: "Living must consist of more than just sustaining oneself; it must also consist of surpassing oneself. If it doesn't, then living is only not dying, and human existence becomes indistinguishable from an absurd vegetation."

Self-Actualization in Action

Boo Bue is a wonderful model of self-actualization; a success by every definition of the word. He is the most highly respected man in Dale Carnegie Training. He achieved outstanding business, personal, and financial success. His major purpose is building and developing people and he has an impressive track record spanning forty years. Here's an example of how Boo worked to bring out the best in me:

He called me one day and asked, "Would you like to make a presentation at our international convention in Houston?"

Would I *like* to? Of course I would; I was thrilled! Speaking to a thousand people from all over the world, people from the largest and most prestigious training organization in the world! Of course I said yes, and for the next two weeks I was walking on air.

Boo and I soon spent a day together making sales calls. After dinner, over coffee, he said something that crushed me: "Byron, I don't want you to go down to Houston unprepared to give that talk and 'shoot from the hip.'" I couldn't believe he had so little faith in me. The next morning I picked him up at his hotel and took him to the airport. We didn't talk. I couldn't look at him. Just before he got on the plane, he handed me a note. It said, "I'm sorry if I hurt your feelings last night. I just know how good you are and I want to be sure you have the kind of successful experience you deserve. I wouldn't have lobbied for you to be on the program if I didn't think you could do it."

I was inspired. I wasn't going to let him down. For the next five months I worked on that presentation. I wrote it and re-wrote it. I delivered it to live audiences and I taped it. I listened to the tape and made changes. I sent Boo a tape, he critiqued it and we made changes. When that December day came for me to deliver the speech at the convention, I was ready. It was a hit! I've never given a better talk before or since. The sustained standing ovation was gratifying. I loved it. I received congratulations from my peers and gained respect from the senior management of the organization, one of Boo's goals for me. It ultimately advanced my career.

When I got back from Houston, a letter from Boo was waiting. It said, "In thirty years of attending international conventions, I have never heard a finer presentation." Then, in a characteristic gesture, he threw down a challenge: "I'll bet the two hundred members of the Chico Rotary Club would be as thrilled as we were to hear that presentation." Well, joining the Rotary Club was outside my comfort zone and he knew it. Because of his encouragement, I eventually joined Rotary and enjoyed many years of fellowship and community service.

After he retired, Boo was repeatedly called upon to travel all over the world, instructing trainers in management and leadership skills. He and his wife, Gretchen, have been married over fifty years, have two children and five grandchildren and are active in their religious community. He mentors a student at the local high school. He has been involved in service clubs from Hawaii to Minnesota to California. He donates thousands of hours speaking to groups, especially youth groups. His life continues to be one of service, making the world a better place. Everyone who knows him admires and respects him. His life is truly a life worth living. He lives by his values and priorities.

Priority Living

If you look at someone's top three priorities and none of them are career related, they are probably in the wrong job. That is why it is so important for us to find the right work to do. Many people do not feel fulfilled in their jobs. If you ask the average person, "Are you doing what you want to be doing five years from now?" you'll probably get a negative answer. Too many people are vocationally disturbed. That is, they are unhappy in their work and they don't know what would make them happy, which is why finding one's purpose is so important.

It is easy to be fooled into thinking we're pursuing the right path because parents, teachers, friends, and popular culture have sold us on thinking, "this is what *I* really want."

For example, I once hired a talented man whom I liked very much, and who had always demonstrated tremendous promise. In the twenty years I'd known him, he had never fully realized that promise.

I knew when I hired him that he had a great track record as a salesman but no experience in management, which requires a different set of skills. I needed a sales manager and thought I could help him develop the necessary skills for the job. I also knew that he was a devout churchgoer and devoted to his family, but I didn't know how much he loved selling.

After he'd been working for me for six months, we met to talk about why he was under-achieving and what I could do to help him. Combined with his devotion to his wife and children and the number of hours he volunteered each week for his church, there just wasn't enough time and focus left to prepare himself for management. He has enviable values. It wasn't until he was forced to tell himself the truth about what he *really* valued—selling—that he told me he couldn't continue trying to become a manager. He resigned with my blessings and went back to selling for his former company and did very well. His life conformed to his values.

Dr. George Winslow Plummer tells us in *Consciously Creating Circumstances*, that our thinking must be focused in order to tap into the power that resides in our subconscious mind.

By now you might be saying, "I've heard all this stuff before. There's nothing new here." You're right. These ideas are thousands of years old, maybe older. I don't claim them as mine. But I've studied as many ideas as I possibly could to help others and myself. I'm passing them on in the spirit of wanting to help you, and I've arranged them in a workable order. I've given credit wherever possible. Perhaps you can consider these ideas a review or memory joggers. Herbert Spencer, the great English educator and essayist, said, "We all need more to be reminded rather than taught."

The Person I Want to Be

Here's a technique I use to organize my thinking and help me clarify my definite major purpose in life. I think you'll find it useful too. I call it, "The Person I Want to Be," a written, idealized description of every aspect of my life as I want it to be. This is really an expansion of the exercise at the end of the first chapter, Vision. In that exercise, you looked ahead five years and painted a preliminary word picture of what your life would look like if there were no limits on your success.

Since then you've been introduced to two more tools, Purpose and Thinking. Now you're in a position to enrich that picture.

In this expanded word picture, describe yourself in terms of the material, artistic, philosophical, behavioral, spiritual, and educational conditions you want. Add the physical, societal, and the familial sides of your life. By developing an *objective* description, as though you're describing the person you most admire in the world, you'll be less tempted to weaken or water-down the picture.

Once this ideal picture is developed, you'll be able to compare what you are actually doing with what you should be doing, as defined by that ideal. It will show you where you need to improve.

In my daily reading, I found that an important part of the exercise was to analyze my motivation in making those needed improvements. At the end of the exercise I felt as though I really knew myself, and as a result I didn't make the mistake of embracing conflicting values. As an unexpected bonus, a powerful, internal gyroscope—one that has enabled me to maintain balance in my life—indirectly grew out of this exercise. You'll read about that and be able to adapt it for yourself in the discussion on affirmations.

Many of the conditions or circumstances in the description of one's ideal life may be effects or behaviors, as opposed to actual goals. And in every case there should be a consistency between one aspect and all others. For example, one could not reasonably expect, within the same description, to find a social life of heavy partying and a lifestyle of physical fitness. Nor could one reasonably expect to spend all their time advancing their career—at any cost—while wanting a balanced family life. This description might include some conclusions as to where one wants to live, as well as to the kind of work he or she wants to do. We'll prosper and be much happier in the right geographic, social, and business atmosphere. Also, we are more apt to exercise priority living; that is, having those things that are most important to us at the top of our to do list.

Focusing our thinking habits serves to clarify our values. It enables us to design a purposeful life. The description should be a living one that changes, broadens, and becomes more ambitious as a person matures. The fundamentals will remain constant, however.

Benefits of Describing Your Ideal Self

The benefits of such a description or mental focus are:

1. It gives you an exciting picture of the person you could be.

2. It sets some ambitious goals for you.

3. It gives you a daily checklist against which you can measure your progress.

4. Daily reading causes the description to be on your mind and as you think, so you are. We'll discuss how to do this in the chapter on affirmations.

5. It keeps you from becoming distracted by temporary, frivolous pursuits, so you can keep your eye on the ball.

Programming Our Subconscious Mind

The next method for using our thoughts to find our major purpose is to program our subconscious mind. The technique is simple. Several times a day, write and ask yourself the question you want answered: "What is my purpose?" Then wait for the answer. The more important the answer is, the more intensity you'll put into your thought. I prefer to write my requests positively, using the first person present tense, as though the problem has already been solved. For example, if one is looking for the answer to the question, "What business am I in?" one might say, "I have a clear, perfect purpose for my life." This is a powerful technique that has worked for others and for me.

Now it's time again to ask and answer some important questions and go into action.

First Essential Tool: Thinking

Questions and Actions

1. What do I think about? What are my top three priorities? Are they the ones I want?

2. What books am I reading? Who are the people with whom I spend my time? Make a list and evaluate it. I heard once that in five years, we will be the same person we are today except for the books we read, the people we meet, and the dreams we dream. I'll give you some great methods in the People and Communications chapters for finding the right kind of people, and what to say to them to cause them to want to spend time with you.

3. Are those the books and the people that will help me develop and express my highest and best self? Will they help me achieve my purpose in life? If not, what changes do I need to make in order to be consistent with the person I aspire to be? What are my dominant thoughts during the day? Note: You might find this difficult to answer if you just sit down to think about your thoughts, so carry a note pad with you and periodically write down what you are doing, reading, or talking about throughout the day. Actions are a reflection of our thought. Review your notes and ask yourself, "Are my thoughts and actions consistent with what I want to do and be? If not, what thought and action do I need to alter in order to be the person I aspire to become?" A week of this kind of periodic analysis should give you a clear picture of your dominant thoughts.

4. List your top three priorities.

5. Write a description of the person you want to be. Compare this description with the ideal life you wrote at the end of the Vision chapter.

Good luck. This exercise can bring about some powerful life-changing experiences.

Goals

"If you have built castles in the air, your work need not be lost, that is where they should be. Now get busy and put foundations under them."

—Ralph Waldo Emerson

When I first set the goal to own my own training company, I knew that achieving it would not be easy because of my competition. There were other candidates, many as qualified as I, who also wanted to own one of these hard-to-come-by franchises. In the face of this kind of competition, I needed to use every skill I'd ever learned.

Goal-Setting in Context

On any given Sunday afternoon during the season you can turn on the television set and see an NFL game in progress. You see the quarterback take the snap from the center and fade back to pass. He spots his open receiver and releases the ball just in time to complete the pass!

You are watching the goal setting process at work. The quarterback is fulfilling his destiny, his purpose in life, to be an NFL quarterback. At the start of the season, his major goal is to win the Super Bowl. For now, his intermediate goal is to win this game. His sub-goal is to score this touchdown. But first, he has to make a first down.

The danger with goal setting, as I see it, is the potential for taking the process out of context. Without the perspective of a larger purpose, goal setting can be sterile, ineffective, and unproductive. Moreover, it can be frustrating. As I mentioned earlier, embracing a definite major purpose is the process of turning oneself over to a powerful, driving inner force that enables even those of us with modest talents—as I consider myself to be—to achieve and persevere in the face of adversity. But a purpose is just a foundation upon which to build our lives. Understanding the psychological effects of having goals enables us to put the goal setting process into a larger, more meaningful context.

Think of your purpose as Emerson's dream castles; a vision of all those things and conditions that constitute a life worth living. Then think of the goals you set as the foundations to make those castles real.

Purpose, Passion and Goals

What a joy it is to meet people who are caught up in a purpose, a cause bigger than the person. Tony Hopson, founded Self Enhancement, Inc., in Portland, Oregon. What an organization! What passion! SEI is dedicated to helping inner-city youth realize their full potential, so you can see why I was interested in them— their mission is so closely allied with mine. SEI's success rate is phenomenal. They graduate 98 percent of students in their program, and 80 percent of them go on to college.

What Tony has contributed to the young people of inner-city Portland will live well beyond his lifetime. His belief and commitment to SEI made his cause Portland's cause, and supporters lined up to help him make his dream come true.

It wasn't like that in the beginning. He faced obstacles and experienced enough disappointment to discourage almost anyone else. But throughout his struggles, he knew that setbacks are merely a part of achieving goals.

Tony Hopson affirmed his vision and belief many times in pursuit of his dream. "I believe the work I do is God's work. It's really the faith I have; that the work we're doing is correct. It's the work I was put on the planet to do."

In a recent interview I asked him if it was the achievement of which he is most proud. He said, "No, not starting the program, but sustaining it for so many years. When my high school team won the state basketball championship, I learned that it's not the goal, it's the journey."

I asked, "Your sons all work at SEI. What would you tell them, or any other young person, who might come to you for advice on achieving their goals?"

He looked me in the eye and said, "I'd tell them to be patient and be true to their mission."

Note how closely Tony's mission, vision, and affirmation conform to the definite major purpose we discussed earlier. But affirmations and vision by themselves didn't achieve his dream, nor will they achieve our dreams for us.

We Must Take Action!

It's necessary to take action and set measurable goals that move us in the direction of making our mission and vision a reality.

Writer Jack London sent nearly six hundred stories to publishers before one was accepted; yet he continued to write and submit because his goal was to be a writer. *He could think of nothing else.* Thinking about his purpose and his goal led to his success. He didn't sit and daydream about writing; his desire and persistence in pursuing his goal finally enabled his work to be accepted.

A modern-day writer, J. K. Rowling, the world's first billionaire author, wrote the first scene of *Harry Potter* on a napkin, and then kept writing. Harry Potter was her passion and completing the Harry Potter saga was her goal.

When Eddie Snow, a California businessman, wants to underscore the importance of getting into action, he draws on his Oklahoma roots by quoting Emerson, with a grin: "Thinkin' don't do it—doin' do it. That's not Ralph Waldo Emerson, it's Jake Emerson of Granite, Oklahoma."

Another of his favorite expressions, which he uses when making a serious point in a speech is, "I didn't come out to preach to you, although Lord only knows some of you need it." I'm not here to preach. In fact, I'll remind you again that neither I nor anyone else can determine how you should live. We are each responsible for creating our own life worth living.

Identifying Goal Areas to Ensure Balance

Creating a life worth living requires balance. Let's identify the important goal-setting areas of our lives. In his autobiography, Benjamin Franklin chose thirteen areas in which he felt he needed to improve and systematically set out on a path of self-development in those areas. After reading his autobiography I was inspired to set goals in these particular areas of my life: Family, Personal Growth, Finances, Health, Community, Spiritual, Education, and Career.

You may have different priorities. Once you have selected the areas, write the answers to some basic questions:

- What do I want to achieve in each of these areas? When do I want to achieve it? How will I know it's been achieved?

- What would indicate a halfway point? What would tell me early on that I'm headed in the right direction?

In the process of answering these questions, set your goals high; most people tend to set their goals too low.

Humor: I was conducting a training program for a group of managers a few years ago and asked each of them to set a goal for the next year. One of the managers, who had an MBA, stood and said, "My goal is to finish my book." I said, "I didn't know you were writing a book." He said, "I'm not. I'm *reading* one!"

Keep in mind that goals are revisable. We can tear them up and write new ones at any time if our priorities change. In fact, goal setting should be an ongoing evaluation process that continues throughout life.

Goal-Setting Techniques

In our description of a goal, we must be absolutely clear about what attainment will look like, in quantifiable terms: How much? How long? How many? By when? In other words, let's describe our goals in such a way that we can measure our progress.

If we can't measure it, we can't manage it.

Being specific and describing our goals in measurable terms is one way to track our progress.

Humor: A traveler riding into Nottingham noticed several bull's-eyes painted on the trees along the roadside with arrows dead in the center of every one. In the town, he stopped at the local pub and asked the innkeeper if he had seen the excellent display of marksmanship and if he knew the archer.

"Indeed I have seen his work and I do know the archer," he said. "In fact, that's him sitting at the end of the bar."

The traveler approached the marksman and was surprised to meet a bleary-eyed old-timer with shaking hands. "You're quite an archer," said the traveler. "I saw your artistry on my way into town. How do you do it?"

The old-timer fixed his drunken eye on the traveler and slurred, "Buy me a pint and I'll show you."

A pint was bought, guzzled down and off they went into Sherwood Forest. The archer took out his bow, put an arrow in it and unsteadily aimed at a group of trees. He let go. The arrow stuck in one of the trees. Then the archer reached in his sack, took out a bucket of paint and a brush and painted a target on the tree, with the arrow dead center in the bull's-eye.

Many people approach life like that archer. Unplanned-for events take place in their life and then they act as though that's the way they planned it all along. I tell my golfing buddies when I slice the ball, "I did that on purpose. I like to approach the green from over there."

Set Deadlines

My experience has been that a date is necessary for attaining a goal because it forces me to be accountable. If I don't set a deadline, I fall into the "someday" syndrome.

For example, a five-year-old boy stood beside his busy father, who was working at his desk and asked, "Daddy, when is someday?" His father replied, "Why do you ask, son?" The little boy said, "Because whenever I ask you when we can go to the park and play, you always say 'someday'."

Someday never comes. Putting a time limit on goal-attainment causes the goal to become a commitment to yourself.

Let's look at an example of a goal for a student entering college.

Ultimate Goal: In four years I have graduated with a minimum of a three-point GPA by June 2013.

Interim Goal: My major is selected by September 1, 2011, and all required courses are completed with 3.3 GPA or better.

First checkpoint: My first academic year is completed by June 1, 2010 with a documented record of three hours of study per week for every credit hour and a GPA of 2.8 or better.

Another example, in the area of fitness, for a thirty-five-year-old woman with a career and limited training time, might read:

Ultimate Goal: I have completed the New York City marathon by November 2010, in a time of three and one-half hours or less.

Interim Goal: I have completed a half marathon by March 1st 2009, in two and one-half hours.

First Checkpoint: One month. I have completed my long/short training schedule six days per week for four weeks and log my progress.

One of the most inspiring examples of successful goal-setting using checkpoints was the breaking of the four-minute mile barrier in track. No one had ever crossed the barrier until Roger Bannister did it on May 6, 1954. It was thought to be humanly impossible, a feat beyond the physical ability of man. But after researching the mechanical aspects of running, Bannister believed it could be done and developed the scientific training methods he needed to achieve his goal.

He then enlisted the assistance of two fellow runners as pacesetters. He also had timers with stopwatches stationed every one-eighth of a mile, as checkpoints, to tell him exactly where he was and if he was on schedule. He instructed his pacesetters take turns running in front of him until the last two hundred yards. Then he took the lead and sprinted across the finish line in 3:59.4 minutes, becoming the first sub-four-minute-miler in history. The myth of the unbreakable four-minute mile was destroyed forever. Two months later, the Australian miler, John Landy, also broke that barrier, proving the barrier to be as psychological as physical. Then, the year following Bannister's record-breaking performance, a number of other runners also broke the barrier, and by the turn of the twenty-first century the record was three minutes, forty-three seconds.

An interesting side note to the Bannister story can help us as we pursue our own goals. Roger was barraged by reporters with the question, "What did it take for you to do it?" His answer: "It's the ability to take more out of yourself than you've got."

The Real Benefit of Setting Goals

The major benefit of setting and attaining goals is not the attainment of the goal per se; the real reward is the person one becomes in the process of attaining the goal. This is dramatically illustrated for us every four years at the Olympic Games, when we see the world's best athletes perform after years of goal setting and preparation. We're inspired when we watch the vignettes shown on television of the sacrifices these young people have made to qualify for the Games. The impact of the discipline and training on their character, personality, and bodies leave lasting impressions on us, whether they win or not.

"The most important thing in the Olympic Games is not to win but to take part, just as the most important thing in life is not the triumph but the struggle." Baron Pierre de Coubertin, President, International Olympic Committee from 1896 to1925.

Consider the two examples above, the college student and the marathoner. At the end of the process of earning a college degree, the student has learned to make mature choices, usually studying versus partying. The same holds true for the marathoner, who no doubt has to pass up not only social opportunities, but must make some temporary adjustments in her work and family life.

What both of these goal achievers discover is a key ingredient of success. That ingredient is delayed gratification. A business executive by the name of Albert E. N. Gray gave a speech some years ago entitled, *The Common Denominator of Success*. He said he'd found the component present in every successful person's life. He said, "Successful people form the habit of doing the things that failures don't like to do." He went on to say that successful people don't like to do those things either, but, "successful people are motivated by pleasing ends, not by pleasing means."

That's why setting goals—and pursuing them energetically and enthusiastically—pays such big dividends. The reward of walking across the stage to receive your diploma. The thrill of crossing the finish line of a race. Realize that the higher the stakes, the greater the reward and the more required of us.

However, with greater reward comes the increased potential for disappointment, which is why so many people set their goals too low. I do know that going for what you perceive to be the top is definitely "the road less traveled," as Robert Frost said. It is the uncommon way. The inconvenient way. It is the way that most people don't want to take because it does require effort.

The critical ingredients in the lives of all the successful people I've met are *action* and *work*. We can sell ourselves on exerting the necessary effort to accomplish our goals by getting a clear mental image of ourselves achieving success. If we do that, we create a commitment that overcomes any discomfort and inconvenience.

One sets a goal with the expectation of a payoff. It is true that we are rewarded for our effort, but the real benefit of achieving a goal is the person we become in the process of attainment. Jennifer James wrote *Success is Not a Destination but a Journey*, in which she, too, makes the point that the benefit one accrues during the journey outweighs the reward at the end.

In 1990, Patricia set a serious athletic goal to finish the Portland Marathon. My wife, until then, had not participated in any athletic event, other than recreational skiing and jogging. She started training. She enrolled in a running clinic and followed the program to the letter. During the nine months before the actual race, she was really tested physically, mentally, and emotionally. She watched as others got discouraged and dropped out of the program, yet she kept running. She teamed up with a running buddy for support and they held each other accountable. They ran early in the morning in the dark and the rain. One day she fell while on a long run in the park, and finished the run with her face, arms, and legs cut and bleeding. She was right on schedule until a major hurdle presented itself two months before the marathon, the most demanding part of the training.

Patricia's mother became seriously ill, and she immediately jumped on a plane and flew to Nova Scotia. She called the local running club to line up a training partner, but there was no one available. She was on her own. That, coupled with her mother's illness, was a perfect excuse for her to bag the whole painful process. But she kept running, by now fifteen to eighteen miles a day; twenty miles on foggy Saturday mornings. She returned to Portland after her mother was discharged from the hospital, and resumed her training schedule with Janet. When the day of the marathon came, she was ready.

Our daughters and I were there to cheer her on at the start and wait for her at the finish. As I saw her cross the finish line, I was filled with pride! I asked her, "Was that achievement of crossing the finish line as rewarding as you expected?"

She said, "Yes it was, but that wasn't the most important benefit. I learned more in the training process about my character than anything else."

"What do you mean?" I asked.

"I didn't quit. I made up my mind that I wouldn't give up my goal of completing the marathon, no matter what. And I didn't."

I was reminded of what James Allen said in *As a Man Thinketh:* "Circumstances do not make the man; they reveal him unto himself." Patricia certainly revealed the depth and strength of her character when faced with extremely challenging circumstances.

We know that our behavior is influenced by our attitudes but don't always recognize that a major influence on our attitudes is skill. For example, a good tennis player might reasonably say, "I'm good at tennis, therefore I enjoy playing tennis and you'll find me on the tennis court whenever I get a chance." The negative side of this thinking might be, "I don't enjoy tennis, therefore I'm no good at it and you'll not likely find me eagerly participating in it." We participate in activities in which we have skill and as a result have a good attitude toward them. To increase our success satisfaction we only need to increase our skill. Malcolm Gladwell illustrates this dramatically in *The Outliers*, in which he talks about the ten thousand hours invested by high achievers to develop their skill.

These examples give us some guidelines for measuring the illusive, unpredictable, serendipitous outcomes of goal setting. These outcomes also provide us with additional motivation and joy when they unexpectedly occur.

In this chapter, we've talked about the rewards of going the extra mile and the effort required to accomplish those rewards. To achieve anything worthwhile, we need to pay our dues—to practice, study, and work—but my experience and studies have shown me that the rewards far outweigh the effort required to achieve them. Most encouragingly, we do not have to be a great deal better than every one else in order to achieve those rewards.

Remember how impressive Mark Spitz's record-setting performance was in the 1976 Munich Olympic Games? His record of achieving seven gold medals stood in Olympic history until Michael Phelps did the impossible in Beijing in 2008 by winning eight. In both cases their winning times were only fractions of seconds faster than the times of the second-place finishers. A little difference makes a big difference.

Tiger Woods is rated the number one golfer in the world and arguably the greatest individual athlete in history because of his dominance in his sport. In 2007, his tournament winnings were

$10,867,052.00, with an average of 69.10 strokes per 18 holes. In ninety-ninth place that same year, Jeff Overton earned $1,009,630.00. His average number of strokes per eighteen holes was 70.10—a mere difference of one stroke. Once again, a little difference made a big difference.

As an additional way to motivate ourselves and increase our benefits in pursuit of our goals, let's consider some questions: "What other benefits might I gain from attaining this goal? What would that mean to me? What sub-goals can I set for myself to attain the major goal I'm after?"

Here's a personal example I remember well: When I set a major goal to own my own training company, I knew I would need a lot of energy, so I started jogging for fitness. I was a heavy smoker at the time and without consciously deciding to quit smoking, I found it to be inconsistent with my fitness goal. My smoking habit just fell away. I lost the desire to smoke. I'd frequently tried to quit before by using will power, but without success. So as a result of one positive action, a multiplicity of related benefits can be achieved.

Let's consider these questions and actions:

Fourth Essential Tool: Goals

1. List the five areas you consider most important in a balanced life. What are five or six major achievements you'd like to be remembered for when you reach the age of retirement?

2. How can you convert these achievements into one-year, five- year, and ten-year goals as they relate to your definite major purpose?

3. How will you measure your progress?

4. What must you do? What positive actions do you need to take in your life right now? What changes do you need to make in order to attain those goals?

5. Visualize yourself as having already taken those positive actions. How do you see yourself behaving and talking? Can you set mutually supportive goals connecting all of those changes?

6. What is one action step you will take immediately to set your goal- setting mechanism in motion? When will you do it?

Now that you've answered these questions, go back and review your description of the person you want to be and rewrite it in specific, measurable, goal-oriented terms.

Congratulations! You've completed the first part of this book and laid the foundation for your success.

This is a perfect time for you to sit down with your mentor, advisor, spouse, or support person. Discuss what you've accomplished so far. Use the feedback from that conversation to revise and update your answers from the Foundations for Success.

Part Two

Mental Tools for Success

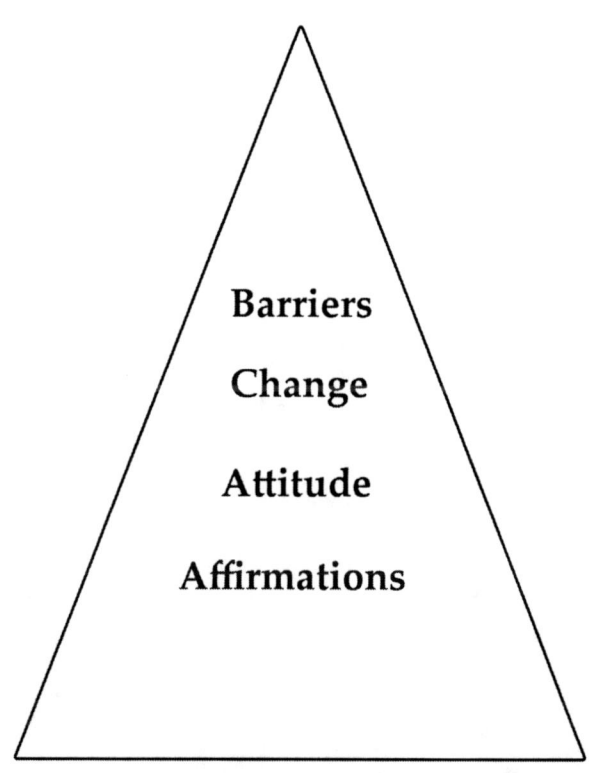

Barriers

Change

Attitude

Affirmations

The Fifth Essential Tool

Barriers

"The only thing we have to fear is fear itself."
—Franklin D. Roosevelt

Self-Doubt

Jack Boland, a minister in Michigan, referred to a phenomenon he called second force. Jack said that almost as soon as one sets a big goal, an equally powerful negative reaction takes place. One thinks of all the reasons why attainment of the goal is impossible: "I don't have what it takes," "Who am I to try to do that?" "Other people are better qualified." Don't let this negative force of self-doubt rob you of energy and destroy your ambition.

Good News

Understanding the existence of second force is really good news for the person who is serious about pursuing any worthwhile goal. Knowing that these thoughts are inevitable gives one the ability to dismiss them for the frauds they are. Many times we give up on our goals before we even try. Shakespeare expressed this perfectly when he said, "Our doubts are traitors and make us lose the good we oft might win, by fearing to attempt." We must constantly remind ourselves of this important concept so we don't lose the momentum necessary for us to achieve our goals.

Our thoughts don't control us; we control our thoughts.

Here's a personal example: for years I had a goal to organize my journals and put them in publishable form, but I always had perfect excuses. I had a family to raise and support, a business to run, and community obligations to fulfill. These things all took time, energy, and focus. I was busy and had plenty of excuses. Actually, the real reason I procrastinated was fear.

Fear

Fear of failure and criticism holds us back; fear of what others might think of us and say about what we've produced. I know from long-time experience of training men and women how devastating fear can be. I also know that it can become a wise teacher if we use fear to our benefit and don't give it control. I'm persuaded that we all face an enormous amount of fear, and the more we challenge ourselves, the more we experience it. Ralph Waldo Emerson counseled us to, "do the thing you fear to do and the death of fear is certain."

That's exactly what I did when I stood on the Kawarau Bridge looking at the water a hundred and twenty-seven feet below me. Certainly the sensation of fear arose, but I observed it, acknowledged it, and reminded myself that I was more than that. Fear is a thing apart from me; I could either let it control me, or I could control it. I chose to be in control and dove off the bridge tethered to an elastic band.

I've had similar experiences—rappelling down the side of a mountain during an executive training program, and many times skiing black diamond runs. I must tell you I didn't have to ski too many of those expert runs to get value from facing my fear. Once or twice a year usually does it. I give you these examples not because I'm a particularly brave guy but to illustrate that my greatest barrier to achievement has been fear. I find the most effective way for me to deal with fear is to confront it, and I believe that is true for all of us.

I witnessed this courageous confrontation of fear in thousands of people over the years in Dale Carnegie classes, when individuals stood before a group to speak. (According to *The Book Of Lists*, people are more afraid of public speaking than of death.) Initially, many were so frightened that they were barely able to complete a short, simple assignment, but as they faced their fear and developed skill, fear disappeared and their effectiveness increased dramatically. They expanded their comfort zone.

The larger our comfort zone, the greater challenges we can handle. We can expand that comfort zone by employing the essential tools in this book and experiencing increased competence in our day-to-day activities. If our comfort zone is too small for the challenges we face, we can become overwhelmed and fail to act.

The Debilitating Effects of Fear

I know this from personal experience. During my adventure in Spain, I went to Geneva, Switzerland, headquarters of the United Nations, armed with a stack of resumes, looking for a job interview.

I poked around various UN agencies looking for opportunities and found one at the International Labor Organization. They were looking for someone to go to Nairobi, Kenya to teach business skills to African businessmen. Since I had a teaching and business background and spoke English, I was their guy. All I needed to do was complete an application, get a security clearance, and I was on my way. Most exciting was the news that I'd be able to take my family with me. It was going to take several months for the application and security check to be completed and since our money was very low, we decided that Patricia should take our daughters to Canada, where they could stay with her family until everything was set.

I kissed them goodbye and put them on a plane. Then fear set in. I was in over my head! "I can't do that job," I said to myself. "I don't have the qualifications. I've overstated my experience. They'll find me out when they start checking. I was overwhelmed. I was paralyzed. I couldn't get the application typed. I couldn't write to request the necessary letters of recommendation. Alone in a big city in a foreign country, I had no confidence and became increasingly depressed as more and more time went by. The worst part was that I couldn't tell my wife that I was blowing this opportunity of a lifetime, so she and our daughters came back to Barcelona in the spring fully expecting to leave for Africa. When I told her I hadn't followed through, it was the lowest point in my life.

I know how incapacitating fear can be, how it can force us to behave in counter-productive ways. During this period I drank too much, ate to excess, and slept late instead of getting things done. Now I recognize that alcohol, food, and sleep are just a few of the devices we use to escape facing ourselves; devices that keep us from being fully awake and conscious. They were futile efforts to cover up the debilitating effects of fear.

I've interviewed a great many people, many of them of significant achievement, and after we'd become comfortable with one another, in almost every case they admitted to experiencing fear. They sometimes called it by another name, but it was fear.

Don't Be Fooled By Me

Don't be fooled by me.
Don't be fooled by the face I wear.
For I wear a thousand masks, masks that I'm afraid to take off, and
    none of them are me.
Pretending is an art that's second nature with me, but don't be fooled,
    for God's sake, don't be fooled.
I give the impression that I'm secure, that all is sunny and unruffled
    with me, within as well as without,
That confidence is my name and coolness my game,
That the water's calm and I'm in command, and that I need no one.
But don't believe me. Please.

My surface may seem smooth, but my surface is my mask.
Beneath this lies no complacence.
Beneath dwells the real me in confusion, in fear, and aloneness.
But I hide this. I don't want anyone to know it.
I panic at the thought of my weakness and fear being exposed.
That's why I frantically create a mask to hide behind,
A nonchalant, sophisticated façade to help me pretend, to shield me
    from the glance that knows.
But such a glance is precisely my salvation, my only salvation, and I
    know it.
That is, if it's followed by acceptance, if it's followed by love,
It's the only thing that will assure me of what I can't assure myself—
    that I am worth something.

But I don't tell you this. I don't dare. I'm afraid to.
I'm afraid your glance will not be followed by acceptance and love.
I'm afraid you'll think less of me; you'll laugh at me, and your laugh
    would kill me.
I'm afraid that deep down I'm nothing, that I'm no good and that you
    will see this and reject me.
So I play my game, my desperate game, with a facade of assurance
    without and a trembling child within.
So begins the parade of masks. And my life becomes a front.
Who am I, you may wonder? I am someone you know very well,
For I am every man and every woman you meet.

—Charles C. Finn

Recognizing this tendency in all of us to hide behind our masks has been useful in helping me drop my own facade. It has helped me to be more honest and to show my true self. As a result, I moved into a better position to help others develop and grow.

Identifying Impediments

Since our intention here is to create the life we dream of living, it's necessary to examine anything that could impede our progress toward that objective. Without placing moral judgments on those potential impediments, let's look at them.

In general, they are any counterproductive involvement with substances, activities, or people that detracts from or interferes with the progressive realization of our worthy ideal. Specifically:

1. **Excessive socializing:** This is one habit that is easy to fall into. Parties, dinners, and shows are all fun, and the more financially successful one becomes, the more accessible they are. If I am busy at club meetings or luncheons or dinner parties all the time, I don't have a lot of time to sit down and face myself.

2. **Desire for undue recognition**: This usually comes from a deep-seated lack of confidence. We try to feel important by saying, "Hey, look at me!" manifested by conspicuous consumption—trying to impress with the size of our cars, houses, jewelry, clothes, or anything we think will make others believe we're special. This desire tends to make us susceptible to flattery and too easily crushed by the criticism of others. People exploiting that desire can also easily manipulate us.

3. **The desire to get something for nothing**: Greed in financial dealings, such as gambling in hopes of hitting it big. Not only are we using money in the least effective way, we are

burning up time and energy that could be better used on priority living.

4. **Sexual attention**: Searching for validation from the attention of the opposite sex. This can lead to inappropriate use of time and money and can lead to the delusion that changing current relationships will cause happiness. Maybe it will, and maybe it won't. More than likely it will address the effect rather than the cause.

5. **Over-consumption of alcohol and drugs**: These are popular methods of escape. Drinking is an accepted part of social and business functions; it is easily abused. The use of drugs, whether legal or not, is increasingly widespread in our society.

6. **Overeating**: Eating has the advantage of being acceptable behavior. When we feel insecure, what better way to ward off that need to escape than by over-indulging in comfort food? Is this why so many business meetings are conducted over lunch: to create a secure, comfortable environment?

7. **Exercise**: Exercise is admirable, unless we overdo it in order to exhaust ourselves, so as not to face reality.

There are myriad ways to escape confronting our discontent and facing ourselves; these examples are illustrative rather than comprehensive. I would suggest that each of us identify and examine our own distractions and excesses and weed out the ones that keep us from attaining our goals.

"The chief cause of failure and unhappiness is trading what we want most for what we want at the moment."

What does it take to overcome these barriers? I wish I'd known the answer, as I lay awake, tossing and turning, agitated to the brink of tears during those terrible nights in Barcelona. I needed to change my perception of my circumstances and myself.

Years earlier, I experienced that shift in self-perception when Jeff DeHaven, my high school football coach, focused on my strengths as a quarterback. I had always thought of myself as too small to be good. He said "You have really fast hands—you can get the plays off quickly." When he said that, a light came on for me and eliminated the erroneous image I had of myself. I remained small but I played better than I would have without that kind of coaching.

One of the most dramatic examples of a shift in self-image took place during a leadership-training program I conducted in Yuba City, California. I'd asked everyone to talk about a memorable experience from his or her childhood. Alex, who had a defiant, tough-guy manner, had told everyone that he'd been a boxer. He was about five feet five inches tall, and feisty. He told of a time when he was eight years old; he and his older brother were teasing the hogs on their farm. "One of the hogs started chasing us. We were laughing, running for the barbed wire fence to escape. I dove through and turned around to see my brother caught on the fence! I raced away because I was scared. Then, a few yards down the path I saw a big stick. I picked it up, ran back to the fence just as the hog reached it, hauled off and hit him hard across the snout. He squealed and took off. My brother got loose and we ran for the house." Alex added quietly, "All my life I've been ashamed of running away when my brother was in trouble."

To me, what he'd just described was incredibly courageous—to return in spite of his fear. I asked the group what they thought of Alex's behavior that day. They all said the same thing: "What courage!" "You must have really loved your brother to endanger yourself like that!"

From that moment on, the most miraculous change came over Alex. His opinion of himself changed; he softened and became more enthusiastic, lighter in his attitudes. By the time he finished the program he had set some new goals—not to prove to other people that he wasn't a coward, but to advance himself in the direction of being the person he'd always wanted to be.

Now it's time for you to go to work with this information.

No one needs to see your answers, so be bone honest with yourself. You might have to dig a little to answer these questions, but it will be worth it.

Fifth Essential Tool: Barriers

Questions and Actions

1. What are some things that get in your way, such as personal habits, behaviors, or counter-productive activities?

2. What can you substitute for them? For example, jogging and exercise replaced my smoking habit when I set the goal of owning a training company. Remember, we said it's impossible to embrace two incompatible beliefs.

3. What are you afraid of? How would you behave if you weren't afraid? How can you shift your perceptions?

4. What's one fear you need to confront to eliminate that barrier? What will you do to confront it? When will you act?

5. What will you do today to eliminate a barrier?

The Sixth Essential Tool

Change

*"There is no sin punished more implacably by nature than
the sin of resistance to change."*
—Anne Morrow Lindbergh

"Do you think it will stop raining?" someone once asked Mark
Twain. "Always has," he replied. He could have given the same answer if he had been asked, "Do you think the world will change?"

Up to this point, I may have given the impression that once
one discovers one's purpose, gets his or her thinker working, sets
some goals, identifies and deals with a few barriers, that he or she
is home free. Not true!

When we discuss self-management, we'll deal in depth with
other ways to manage change. For now, we want to understand the
nature of change and our relationship to it.

Change takes place at unprecedented speed today. In order for
us to create this life worth living we're pursuing, we need to learn
how to live and operate in a changing world. This chapter is designed to help us develop awareness of change and its role in our
success.

It was estimated that in the year 1750, the total accumulated
knowledge of mankind had doubled from the time of the birth of
Christ. Imagine—it took 1750 years to double!

Then it doubled again in 1900, a period of only one hundred
and fifty years. The next doubling took place in 1950—a mere fifty

years, then again in 1968, only eighteen years later. Since then, the rate has been doubling too rapidly to calculate.

The Los Angeles Times reported on a USC study on what the researchers called half-life obsolescence in the professions. They borrowed the term from nuclear physicists, who used it to describe the systematic deterioration of nuclear particles. According to the study, a student graduating from a university will be fifty percent obsolete in his field in five years time unless he keeps pace with the changes in that profession. In addition to underscoring the rapid rate of change, this study is a strong argument for life-long learning.

I repeatedly heard complaints from my clients about the difficulties they faced while trying to remain current in their fields. They told me about spending evenings and weekends with briefcases filled with literature on new developments. More often than not I heard, "I'm not able to keep up."

Consider the twentieth century alone. In little more than three generations, we went from horse-and-buggy transportation to space travel. We moved from the invention of the radio and telephone, to television, the Internet, and instant communication around the world. Look through your mind's eye at the world your grandfather or great-grandfather. Consider how today's world would appear to them.

With technological advances in every field, the world might be almost unrecognizable to them, yet most of us have grown up with change. We take many new developments for granted. We are usually undisturbed by these changes as long as they are incremental. We hardly notice them; in the same way a frog in a pan of water doesn't notice a gradual increase in heat from a fire under the pan. He will sit there without moving until he dies. Unlike the frog, as long as change is gradual, human beings have the ability to assimilate and adapt to new information.

A couple of generations ago, futurist Alvin Toffler coined the term "future shock," the shattering stress and disorientation that is induced in individuals by subjecting them to too much change over a short time. We wake up one morning and find the world different.

Suddenly we feel like a stranger in a strange land. When traveling to different countries, we experience rapid cultural change. Different customs, mores, attitudes, behaviors, foods, and lifestyles are as disconcerting as they are fascinating. I always go through a period of re-adjustment when I return home after spending long periods of time in other countries. For example, in the United States dinner is usually eaten in the early evening; in Spain, dinner at ten or eleven o'clock is considered normal. In third world countries, the cultural differences are even more dramatic. If the disruption is only temporary, we know things will be back to normal when we get home, and are reassured.

But as we move inexorably toward an increasingly changing world, we are forced to face the realization that some things are not ever going to be normal again. Thomas Wolfe said, in his book by the same name, "you can never go home again."

The challenge for us in the twenty-first century is adjusting to the advances that happen so fast that they cause a paradigm shift, in the words of Joel Barker, futurist and author of *Future Edge: Discovering the new Paradigms of Success*. When a mental construct is destroyed and what we always believed is no longer true, we have gone through a paradigm shift. The word paradigm comes from the Greek *paradeigma*, which means model, pattern, or example. Barker states, "A paradigm is a set of rules and regulations that does two things: It establishes or defines boundaries, and it tells you how to behave inside the boundaries so as to be successful."

Paradigms define our world and help us make sense of what we see happening around us. It is those shifts—when what we previously believed to be true is no longer true—that throw us off balance and represents a serious barrier to our success. Understanding paradigms becomes important for us in creating our own successful life.

It was a universally held belief that the world was flat until Columbus left on his courageous voyage in 1492 with three tiny sailing ships. When people heard he had found, not a new route to India but a previously undiscovered continent, a paradigm shifted. Major Yuri Gagarin became the first man to travel in space, defying long-held beliefs that it was an impossibility—that was a paradigm shift. Barker went on to say, "when a paradigm shifts, everything goes back to zero." Everybody looks at the new model or paradigm without the previously secure references points.

Certainly the most dramatic paradigm shift in our lifetimes is recognized simply as 9/11. When that terrible tragedy struck, a change took place in the mentality of the American people and we will never be the same. Those rapid and dramatic changes have created a whole new set of rules by which we must play. For example, let's say we were to change the rules of baseball. Under the new rules, when the batter hits the ball and begins to run, the bases move. That's today's environment.

"Change is the basis of progress and growth," Disraeli said. "In a progressive country, change is constant, change is inevitable."

How do we successfully react to change?

Security Touchstones

The world is not a static place, although there are aspects of our lives that have a feeling of permanence and it is important to recognize the difference between the two. I recently experienced security when I went to a high school reunion. Many of the old familiar places were still present in my hometown, and they brought a flood of memories. I savored the special quality of visits with friends I hadn't seen in many years. Those relationships possess a singularity that was not lost by the passing of time. It is important to recognize that security and familiarity in an increasingly mobile society. Unlike our forefathers, many of us do not live in same communities in which we grew up. There is value in experiencing things that do not change, or change very little. The value lies in having a sense of permanence, in contrast to the transient world of the twenty-first century.

As we think about change, it is helpful to remind ourselves of the Serenity Prayer:

"God grant me the serenity to accept the things I cannot change, the courage to change the things I can; and the wisdom to know the difference."

Jude Theibert is a perfect illustration. Jude and JoAnn, his wife, are two friends who represent security touchstones when I visit my hometown.

Jude and JoAnn have been happily married for over forty years and have raised five wonderful children, all of whom, by their actions and achievements, are demonstrating the high values learned from their parents. Jude has always been respected for his leadership abilities, humility and caring attitude. A West Point graduate, retired army officer and businessman, with friends and admirers all over the country, he naturally gravitates to a position of leadership in every organization and association to which he belongs. When I am with him, I can't help but notice how happy and fulfilled he is.

However, Jude has had to accept a change in his life that most of us can't begin to imagine. On the last night before finishing his tour of duty in Vietnam, while on a search and destroy mission as an American advisor to a Vietnamese infantry battalion, he stepped on a land mine. He instantly lost one of his legs just below the knee. He accepted his fate immediately and never indulged in self-pity. He told me that the very first thoughts that went through his mind as he looked at his leg was, "'Well, you can't do anything about that' and I became more concerned about losing the other leg or bleeding to death." I asked him how it was possible to deal with an event that was clearly a life-changing disaster with such an attitude of acceptance. He said, "I realized it could have been much worse; I could have lost both legs or even been killed. Later, as I was going through rehabilitation, I thought about JoAnn and my children and realized that I was so much better off than a lot of others. That got me through rehab and enabled me to get on with my life."

What an inspiration Jude's experience represents! Most of us don't have to face such traumatic and dramatic changes.

To be successful, we must understand, anticipate, and adapt to change. Nate McMillan, head coach of the 2008-2009 NBA Portland Trailblazers took the team from twenty-one to fifty-four wins, by changing the way he related to the players. According to his values, he is an early riser, prefers soft, relaxing music, and enjoys reading books. The players, on the other hand, like to sleep late, listen to hip-hop, and play video games. In order to lead these young men effectively, Nate took them on retreats, listened to them, respected them, and in order to communicate, he began sending them text messages, rather than using the telephone. He said, "Nobody picks up their phone any more, but if you send a text message you get an answer right away. It's a whole different generation." Rather than insisting on doing things his way, Nate adapted and adjusted his style to be a more effective coach.

Now it's time to ask ourselves some questions and take some actions.

Sixth Essential Tool: Change

Questions and Actions

1. What major changes have you experienced; marriage, divorce, the death of a loved one, job change, moving, the birth of a child, a promotion?

2. How have you been affected by those changes?

3. What have you learned about yourself as a result? How are you different now?

4. What would you like to do more of, less of, or differently, to meet future changes?

5. What's one thing you can do today to deal more effectively with any negative effects change has had on you? Reconnect with your family and friends? Visit your birthplace or hometown? Look for things that are secure and permanent in your life.

6. Where do you need to adapt or adjust to your changing environment?

Attitude

"The greatest discovery of my generation is that human beings can alter their lives by altering their attitudesof mind."

—William James

For years I've studied the role of attitude in the search for success. We've all known people whose attitudes are so negative they can't find anything positive to say. Others have an aura that brings a smile to your face when you see them. These are people who take control of their thoughts. I'd like you to meet such a person now.

Counting Our Blessings

As I entered the front door of the YMCA in Toledo, Ohio, a short, disabled man wearing a rumpled, cast-off suit greeted me. He said, "Hi, my name's Schroeder. What's yours?" His speech was slurred, his left arm hung uselessly by his side and he dragged an atrophied left leg along as he limped toward me. His smile was lopsided and he adorned it with a poorly groomed mustache. All in all, he was one of the most unattractive people I've ever met.

But my distaste disappeared as I got to know Bob Schroeder over the next year. He turned out to be one of the most beautiful people I've ever known—a warm, generous, supportive friend. When I left for work in the morning, he'd call out in a cheerful voice, "Have a nice day, Byron!" And when I came home late— tired and discouraged after working all day—he'd be sitting in the big, oak chair in the lobby. He'd ask, "How was your day, Byron?" He wasn't just being polite ... he really wanted to know. So I'd sit down and tell him about my day and he'd listen and ask questions. I always felt better after visiting with him.

I learned that Bob's physical impairments were the result of being stricken with polio as a baby. He had a small pension, which he supplemented by pushing a broom and doing some odd jobs for companies around the Y. He was too proud to go on welfare and become a ward of the state.

Sometimes on Sunday afternoons I'd go with him to one of the many neighborhood restaurants he frequented. He knew every server and maitre'd. Sometimes we went to Bud and Luke's Restaurant where there was always a long line. Bob would limp up to the front of the line, smile and say, "Hi, Harry. How's your golf game coming? Have you managed to break 100 yet?" The maitre'd, guarding the entrance with a big red rope, always smiled back and after a few minutes of bantering, he'd say, "Come on in. I've got a table for you." I'd just shake my head. This guy was loved wherever he went.

I was sitting with him in his room one evening when he took off his thick, heavy, built-up shoe. I could see that his foot was red and painfully swollen. "Bob, doesn't that hurt?" I asked.

He replied, "Sometimes the pain is so bad I can hardly stand it."

"You'd never know it to be with you," I said. "You're always so cheerful. How do you do it?"

I still remember his answer: "Other people" he said.

"How do you mean?"

He said, "I find that when I'm interested in others and put them first, I don't have time to think about myself."

What an inspiration Bob was for me. In constant pain, scraping to make ends meet ... yet to be with him, you'd think he had everything in the world. Bob's attitude made my trivial, day-to-day inconveniences seem petty by comparison. I've never forgotten that valuable example.

That lesson was reinforced for me again when I read an interview with the late Dana Reeve, (wife of Christopher Reeve). The contributions that the courageous couple made as advocates for the disabled were impressive and inspiring as they struggled with their own challenges.

We can use the same strategy to deal with our own adversity that Dana used to sustain herself: "There's a formula Chris and I used all the time. When you least feel like it, do something for someone else. You forget about your own situation. It makes me feel better when things are too hard for me," she said.

People like Bob Schroeder and Dana Reeve have made me appreciate what I have, and have prompted me to include the counting of my blessings during my daily meditations.

Some years ago I found a poem that said it all so elegantly.

The World Is Mine

Today upon a bus, I saw a girl with golden hair.
She seemed so gay; I envied her, and wished that I were half so fair.
I watched her as she rose to leave and saw her hobble down the aisle.
She had one leg and wore a crutch, but as she passed, a smile.
O God, forgive me when I whine, I have two legs and the world is
    mine.

Later on I bought some sweets; the boy who sold them had such
    charm.
I thought I'd stop and talk awhile; if I were late t'would do no harm.
And as we talked he said, "Thank you sir, you've really been so kind.
It's nice to talk to folks like you. Because, you see, I'm blind."
O God, forgive me when I whine, I have two eyes and the world is
    mine.

Later, walking down the street, I met a boy with eyes so blue.
But he stood and looked and watched the others play,
It seemed he knew not what to do.
I paused, and then I said, "Why don't you join the others, dear?"
He looked straight ahead without a word; then I knew, he could not
 hear.
O God, forgive me when I whine, I have two ears and the world is
 mine.

Two legs to take me where I go,
Two eyes to see the sunset glow,
Two ears to hear all that I should know.
O God, forgive me when I whine.
Why, I am blest indeed, for this world is mine.

—Dr. Tennyson Guyer

It's important we count our blessings if we want to have a positive attitude. Most successful people make a habit of saying thank you for the gifts they've been given. The major blessings in my life for which I am grateful are: life, health, love, happiness, prosperity, and full self-expression (By this I mean the ability to use the abundance of talents I have been given.)

Yes, as I said, I'm grateful.

Making Our Blessings Count

It's important to count our blessings, but it's more important to make our blessings count.

Each of us are born with unique talents and given gifts that are not always obvious to us. Sometimes they are hidden and must be uncovered and developed.

I further believe it is our responsibility to do something with the gifts we've been given, to make the most of them and to treat those talents as a sacred trust. Ultimately, through action, it is our responsibility to make the most of those talents and gifts.

Humor: Here's a wonderful story to illustrate this point: A minister traveling through the countryside stopped to admire a beautiful, well-kept farm; every vegetable row was weeded and healthy-looking. He saw the farmer standing nearby and said, "This is a bountiful farm the Lord has blessed you with." "Yes," said the farmer, wiping the sweat from his brow, "And you should have seen it when the Lord had it all to himself."

Attitude Toward Personal Growth

In order to make our blessings count and to use our potential talents, we must continually assess our strengths and weaknesses. Then we can determine where we need to develop. When we experience growth, our self-esteem grows and our attitude becomes increasingly positive. It gives us a competitive edge.

Personal growth is a matter of mental attitude. Any serious student of success needs to make personal growth a priority. It is a key factor in career success, according to Gwen Crowell, in management and leadership development for RBC Royal Bank in Halifax, Nova Scotia. "People who set goals at the bank seem to realize the link that exists between their growth and their success," Crowell said.

Growth

I never want to be what I want to be,
There's always something out there yet for me.
Now I get a kick out of living in the here and now,
Yet I never want to think I've learned the best way how.
There's always a higher hill with a better view,
Something to be learned I never knew
And before my days are ended, lord, please,
Never fully fill my cup.
Just let me keep on growing—up ... up ... up.

Author Unknown

Seeing Humor in Life

Humor: A negative guy walks into a restaurant one morning with a sour look. A cheerful waitress greets him: "Good morning sir. What would you like?"

He replies, "I'll have two eggs—one scrambled and one over easy. I don't like my toast burnt, my hash browns overcooked, or my coffee cold. And I'm in a hurry."

"Yes sir, right away," she smiles. In the kitchen, she whispers to the cook, "We've got the most negative, demanding customer that we've ever had out there."

The cook says, "Let's throw him a curve and fix his breakfast exactly the way he wants it—so he won't have anything to complain about."

They did and delivered it to his table in record time. She put the plate down in front of him. It was a work of art, everything hot and neatly positioned on the plate.

"Here you are, sir. I hope you find everything satisfactory."

He looked at the plate with a sour look and said,

"You scrambled the wrong egg."

That's the kind of attitude we want to avoid when in pursuit of our goals, and I'd suggest that those are the kind of people we want to avoid because of the effect they have on our attitudes.

Humor: A fellow walks across the Golden Gate Bridge in San Francisco when he spots a guy up on the railing getting ready to jump. He yells, "Hold it! Things can't be that bad. Let's talk about it."

So they sit down to talk. After fifteen minutes they get up and both jump.

Well, that's an exaggeration, but negative people can have a negative effect on our attitudes and drag us down with them.

By now you have probably figured out that I believe a sense of humor to be part of a constructive, positive mental attitude.

Attitude and Perception

The Oxford dictionary defines attitude as: opinion; a way of thinking. Orientation and outlook are a couple of synonyms. That's the context in which I'm using the word. Attitude can really color our outlook: two people looking at the same situation create entirely different perceptions of reality.

Negative- and positive-minded attitudes populate our world. I remember a couplet from my childhood: "The optimist fell ten stories and at each window bar, he called in to his friends, 'I'm all right so far.'"

Okay, maybe that is taking optimism too far but it does make the point. Perhaps a better example might be: "Two men look out from prison bars, one sees the mud, the other the stars."

It's all a matter of how we choose to look at the world. We can choose to look at a situation either positively or negatively, coloring our worldview as a result. Let's be positive!

One cold, rainy Saturday morning in December, five-year-old Ana and I went out to spend some quality time together. This particular day, in spite of the weather, Ana wanted to go to the Baskin Robbins ice cream store and then to the little bookstore next door. Happily eating her ice cream cone, browsing in the bookstore, she found a special little book called *Pat The Bunny*. She was truly enthusiastic about her find and bubbled over with excitement as she showed me each page and explained it to me. I paid for the book, took her by the hand and we walked outside.

I turned my collar up against the cold rain, thinking, "I'm tired, it's cold, and this is not the most fun I've ever had."

Just then, Ana squeezed my hand and when I looked down into her glowing face, she exclaimed, "What a beautiful day!" At that moment, I understood what attitude was all about.

It's not about your circumstances; it's the way you choose to be in whatever circumstance you find yourself.

Thirteen years later, after Ana went off to college, I found the book. I still keep it, along with the warm memory of that special time with her and the valuable lesson she taught me.

Here's a story to illustrate this point: A young man walks down the road and approaches an old man sleeping in front of the gates to a village. He roughly punches the old man on the shoulder and says, "Wake up, old man! Tell me, what kind of people live in this village? I'm looking for a new place to settle."

"Well I'll be glad to tell you," the old man said, "but first tell me what kind of people lived in the village you used to live in."

The young man replied, "They were awful—liars, cheaters, and hypocrites. I hated them. I'm glad to be rid of them. I hope I never see them again."

"Well, I'd keep moving if I were you," said the old man, "you'll find the same kind of people here."

The negative young man moved on and the old man went back to sleep.

A short time later, another young man approached the old man, gently nudged him and said, "Forgive me for disturbing you, sir, but I'm looking for a new place to call home. Would you be kind enough to tell me—what kind of people live in this village?"

The old man asked as before, "I'd be glad to tell you, but first tell me what kind of people lived in the village you came from?"

"Oh, they were wonderful people," said the young man, "loving, kindly, caring, and generous. I love those people. I'll really miss them."

"Well, I can tell you quite honestly, you'll find the same kind of people in this village. You'll be welcome here." the old man replied.

I never think of that story without asking, "What kind of people am I meeting and doing business with?" and, "Does my assessment of them say more about my attitude than it does about those people?" I know it has a lot to do with the quality of my life and the degree to which I am creating a life worth living.

Choosing Our Attitudes

Our attitude determines the quality of our lives, and we can choose it at every given moment. On his ninetieth birthday, a reporter asked the great financier Bernard Baruch, "How does it feel to be ninety years old?" He replied with a twinkle in his eye, "Great, when you consider the alternative!" There's always an alternative, and sometimes one looks a lot better than the other.

Humor: A guy is struggling down the road carrying a big sack with all his problems in it. Finally he can't take it any more, so he throws the sack down on the road. "Man," he says, "I wish I was dead."

Sure enough the angel of death descends, lands right next to him and says in a deep voice, "You called?"

"Yeah," says the guy, quickly, "Give me a hand getting this sack back up on my shoulders, will ya?"

I'd be willing to bet that if you and I and everybody else in the world threw all of our problems in a big pile in the middle of a field, and looked them over trying to find a better deal or an easier life, we'd end up taking our own back. They'd still be problems, but at least we're familiar with them.

The Effect of Attitude on Actions

John Ralston, former head football coach for the Denver Broncos, tells a wonderful story about this kind of attitude. When John first went to Denver, the Broncos had never had a winning season. In fact, the only reason the Bronco fans had to cheer was the outstanding performance of their star running back, Floyd Little. John once asked Floyd, "How do you do it—be so strong and positive every time you carry the ball, game after game, year after year?"

Floyd's answer was, "Well, I'll tell you, coach. I've been playing football for twenty years, and every time my number is called and I'm down in that three-point stance, I give myself the same self-talk: 'Floyd, this might be the last time you ever carry the ball—what are you going to do with it?'"

That's a question I have internalized. Any time I get ready to do anything of consequence: give a talk, teach a class, or go to an important meeting, I ask it. It has worked well in reminding me to do my best.

My brother Dick made a life-long habit of doing everything with excellence. After a successful career as a sales executive, he always served as a model and a hero for me. At a surprise retirement party his company gave him a few years ago, the people who spoke testified to a man who operated with kindness, skill, and unswerving integrity in everything he did. It's not by accident that he developed his attitude, virtues, and ethics. He was active in his church, a loving husband, a caring father, and a loyal friend. He developed an attitude that contributed to a rich, satisfying life.

We can also fall into the habit of creating the wrong attitudes by giving ourselves negative self-talks, causing us to perform poorly.

Perry Williams, a professional golfer and amateur philosopher, spoke of the role of attitude in achieving success. "Here's my take on it," he said. "The way you achieve success is as important as achieving it."

"Yesterday I played Baviera golf course and I hit two bad shots. Still, I chipped it on to within two yards of the hole and putted it in for par. If I had allowed myself to become discouraged because of those first two shots, I wouldn't have been able to focus on the next two shots, the way I needed to. I was contented with all four of those shots. I didn't get depressed when I hit the first two, and I didn't get overly elated when I hit the next two. You see, I agree with Bob Rotella, the golf psychologist, who says golf is not a game of perfect. You've got to be able to accept birdies and bogies with the same attitude."

Perry's contentment is an effective and productive attitude that is worth pursuing to help us to achieve the quality of life we want.

Contentment comes from knowing and accepting yourself as you are, and with what you do. It comes from knowing that you are at all times striving to be your best self, using and developing all your talents. For this reason, I stress the importance of values, balance, and knowing yourself. I keep a reminder posted on the wall next to my desk, which reads, "Happiness is savoring what you have rather than longing for what you don't have."

Attitude and Success

Over and over, I've read references to the relationship between attitude and achievement, until I've come to believe it may be the most important ingredient in achieving success in any field.

Joe Nicholson is an example of someone with an attitude of success. Joe was a retired, successful businessman and investor. During his career, he and his team trained tens of thousands of people in the Dallas area to develop winning attitudes and leadership skills. We talked about the factors that contribute to people's success in life. Anyone who has had as distinguished a career as Joe would have sound advice. "What advice would you give your nine-year-old godson?" I asked Joe.

"Don't be timid," he said, after thinking about my question for a few minutes.

"Why do you say that?" I asked.

"Well," he said, "the times when I overcame my timidity and fear and charged ahead have paid the biggest dividends."

"Give me an example."

"Okay, one day early in my career, I was walking down the street in Fort Worth, and I saw on the marquee of a hotel that Frank Bettger would be speaking to a group of insurance people that day. Bettger was a legend, both as a leading insurance professional, motivational speaker, sales trainer, and author of *How I Raised Myself From Failure to Success in Selling*.

"'Wow, Frank Bettger!' I said to myself. I'd admired him for years and I would have loved to meet him, but I wasn't in the insurance business and didn't know anyone who would invite me. It was scary to think about going in cold, but I couldn't pass up the opportunity.

"I overcame my fear, walked in, and introduced myself to Mr. Bettger. I explained that I didn't have any business being there, but I wanted to hear him speak. He was flattered by my enthusiasm and invited me to sit in.

"His talk was great. He used the example of an old-fashioned medicine man using nothing but pure enthusiasm to sell his bogus wares. His point to the group of insurance professionals was: If a medicine man can sell pure hokum with enthusiasm, think what you can do using that same kind of enthusiasm to sell a product that really benefits people.

"I loved the idea and told him I'd like to use it in my own speaking. He gave me permission and I have used it for years. A lot of people have heard that message and benefited by it. Frank, as I came to call him, wrote to me periodically and sent me copies of his new books as they came out. We stayed in touch until he died. I never would have had the rich experience of his influence in my life if I had given in to my timidity and backed away from that golden opportunity."

In that story Joe gave me two powerful examples of the effects of attitude on behavior and the rewards that follow when we manage our attitudes.

The first was Joe's attitude in overcoming his timidity, and the second was Frank Bettger's attitude of enthusiasm.

Here are some questions and actions for you to take.

Seventh Essential Tool: Attitude

Questions and Actions

1. Where would you rate your attitude on a daily basis? Rate yourself on a scale of one to ten. How would the people you spend the most time with rate you? Ask them.

2. Do you make it a practice to maintain and project a positive, optimistic attitude?

3. What's keeping you from being as positive about your life as you'd like to be?

4. What are the benefits of maintaining a positive mental attitude? Take a minute right now to start a list of five ways in which you will benefit by becoming even more positive than you are right now.

5. Have you noticed the effect of your attitude on your achievements?

6. What things will you do, starting today, to insure your development of the upbeat mental attitude that others find attractive and that contributes to your success?

The Eighth Essential Tool

Affirmations

"To understand the heart and mind of a man, look not at what he's done but what he aspires to be."

—Kahlil Gibran

How to Achieve a Goal

Goals, goals, goals! If ever I needed achieve a goal, this was it! Here I was, stranded in Barcelona with no money and no chance of getting any, as far as I could tell. Somehow I had to raise enough to get my family and I back to California. I calculated I needed $500. It might as well have been $500,000 for all the hope I had of finding it. I didn't know what to do, I was sick with worry, and I couldn't figure a way out of my dilemma. I had been caught up in merely surviving the whole eighteen months I'd been pursuing, what I could only characterize as "Byron's folly." What had I been thinking? I hadn't stayed in close touch, written, or telephoned my family or any of my friends. My silence made a request for a loan more than a little problematic.

Then, one afternoon as I was poking around in my briefcase, I came across a little twenty-four-page booklet I'd picked up some years before. The name of the booklet was *It Works*. The author identified himself only as R.H.J. The book promised readers anything they wanted if they followed the simple three-step program outlined. I was desperate. Even though it sounded too good to be true, I decided to try it.

In brief, it suggested that the reader write out their goal, read it three times a day and think about it as much as possible during the day, with a positive expectation of achieving it. No problem for me; I could think of nothing else. The difference was that the problem became a goal. I went to the airline office and booked a flight to New York for the four of us, using my maxed-out credit card to hold the seats. They agreed to not to process the charge since I'd be paying cash and would bring the money in the next week. (The instructions in the book said to proceed as though the goal was already completed.) I went about my daily business with my urgent request in mind but without any desperation, as the author had suggested. I remember sitting in the plaza in the Barrio Gotico thinking, "I have the $500 I need to get my family back to the US."

One day I had an inspiration. Eduardo Criado was an acquaintance and local businessman, whom I'd met a few times, although we weren't really close friends. My inspiration, not based on any sensible logic, was to go to see Eduardo and ask him to lend me the money I needed. I went to his office in the Ritz Hotel; he greeted me warmly and invited me to sit down. "How's your writing and your college research project coming along?" he asked.

"Very well," I said, with my fingers crossed. "But I've gone as far as I can here and it's time to go home."

He surprised me by asking, "Is there anything I can do to help you?"

I sucked in a deep breath and said, "Yes, I need to borrow some money. A lot of it!"

"How much?"

I said, "30,000 pesetas."

He looked at me for what seemed an eternity, and then he said, "That *is* a lot of money." I didn't say anything. I just looked at him and waited another eternity. I remember, even now, the silence of his office. I felt my heart beating and was sure he must have been able to hear it. He spoke first, "*Bueno*, come here on Saturday afternoon and I'll have it for you." I thanked him profusely and floated out of his office with overwhelming relief and elation.

On Saturday, he greeted me with a big smile and handed me a fat envelope bulging with thousand-peseta notes. I took from my briefcase an American-style promissory note, elaborately written in my best legalese. It read, "I, Byron E. Thompson, hereafter called the 'Party of The First Part,' do forthwith solemnly swear to repay to Eduardo Criado, 'Party of The Second Part,' the amount of 30,000 pesetas, at 10 percent interest, no later than six months from the above date."

I handed it to Eduardo, explaining what it was. He tore it up without looking at it and said, "*Por favor,* Byron, that is not necessary. There is no interest charged between friends. Just write down when you'll pay me back." So I took a piece of his stationary and committed to pay it back in six months. I've never forgotten Eduardo's generosity and belief in me.

An Important Lesson in Success

The most important lesson I learned during these trying times was the effectiveness of turning our requests over to our subconscious minds. Focusing on the goal with a great degree of intensity and faith in the power within us sets us up to succeed. I reasoned that if this method worked to achieve short-term emergency projects, like raising the money to get home, it would also work to help me achieve my long-term goals. Rhonda Byrne talks about the same method of achieving goals in her best-selling book and video, *The Secret.*

Using Affirmations to Achieve Big Goals

The creation of the more complex, holistic goal of becoming the person I wanted to become would require more long-term subconscious mind programming. Earlier, we discussed the values-clarification process, or "the person I want to be" technique. Coupled with our goals, that technique is a method of warding off discouragement and focusing on our purpose over a long period of time.

Since goal setting is a logical, left-brain activity, I began meditating to access my creative right-brain thinking. I didn't receive any training in meditation; I just sat down in a quiet place, relaxed, cleared my mind, and allowed thoughts to drift in. All my life I'd been thinking in a vague way about success and goals. I needed a sharper, more complete focus and a way of staying in balance. So, along with my definite major purpose in life, I wrote down several affirmations.

Definition of Affirmations

My definition of an affirmation is: a solemn declaration that one states to oneself as though it were an accomplished fact.

Affirmations are intensely personal and private. When we know a person's aspirations in depth, that person becomes incredibly transparent. A person's perceived weaknesses become evident when they voice their affirmations. After all, one wouldn't affirm the possession of a positive quality if they already possessed it. The creation of powerful, usable affirmations is serious business and cannot be undertaken superficially.

However, my desire to assist you and make this book valuable for you is so strong that I'll share mine with you (along with some explanatory comments). The following is an excerpt from my journal:

My Definite Major Purpose in Life

1. To facilitate the growth and development of the maximum number of people through the expansion of their self-concept so as to bring about an improved behavioral change.

2. To serve as a hero or model for others and to assist them in becoming heroes or models.

3. To accelerate the process of personal evolution through the development of my own and others' human resources.

4. To make a difference in the world by developing a new breed of self-actualizing individuals who take responsibility for the condition of the world by participating in the above process.

Affirmations

I am a warrior—I choose.

(The word warrior has a special meaning for me. I've concluded that we either control our habits or they control us. I am in awe of the samurai warriors' ability to exercise self-mastery, since I've never felt self-discipline to be one of my strengths. I added, *I choose* because I'm aware that our daily lives are made up of constant opportunities to choose a course of action rather than to be at the effect of our circumstances.)

I am totally self-supporting, self-directed and responsible for everything in my life.

(I detected in myself a tendency to be dependent on others; to find fault with others for my failures and shortcomings. I needed to take charge of my actions and face the fact that I am the creator of everything—good *and* bad—in my life.)

I am orderly and disciplined in everything I do. I keep organized, accurate records of my money and time.

(I have a tendency to overlook details and miss fine points. I've made some progress, but I still needed to improve in this important area of self-discipline.)

I am an effective planner, goal setter, and achiever.

(Perhaps related to orderliness, I knew I must have structure on a regular basis in order to ward off being a dreamer. I needed to set goals with specific timelines and commit myself to following through and achieving them.)

I am in perfect physical and psychological health.

(To achieve any kind of significant success, I was going to have to work hard. I needed to have stamina and a healthy mental attitude.)

My weight is at the ideal level and I am physically fit and athletic.

(I worked to control my weight and have a body that would serve me in achieving my goals.)

I am a loving, considerate, and effective father and husband.

(I love my wife and children and want to keep my commitment and devotion to them conscious at all times. I've seen enough examples of businessmen who were successful in their work but neglected their families. I wanted to lead a balanced life.)

I am financially solvent and I effectively manage an ever-increasing estate that is sufficient to supply my family and I with all we want. There is always plenty to donate to charity, and we do.

(I know that a strong financial base is important, both for the present and the future. Money is one of the majors in life and I've always had a tendency toward extravagance.)

I am an exceptionally effective businessman, operating in such a way as to set an example for others to follow.

(If I was going to help the maximum number of people, I would have to multiply myself through others. I needed to be an effective manager, executive, and businessman.)

I am an outstanding member of my community and make a significant contribution to the quality of life in it.

(As one who benefited from doing business in my community, I knew I needed to give back.)

I have a perfect balance of spirituality and materiality in my life.

(I've known people who are out of balance one way or the other. I wanted balance.)

Your Inner Gyroscope

These daily reminders, repeated during my morning meditations, helped keep me in balance; in the same way a gyroscope works. When I was leaning too far in one direction, my internal compass would guide me back to center. It's not possible for anyone to ever be totally in balance, as different influences and necessity pull us off-center, but I do believe that I've been more true to myself through the repetition of these affirmations. If you develop your own and use them, they'll serve you well. They keep us focused on those things that are most important to us, and on asking for the right things in the right way.

Humor: An atheist is walking in the woods and hears a noise behind him. Turning around, he sees a big black bear standing on his hind legs, about to attack. He takes off running through the woods and, looking back over his shoulder, sees the bear gaining on him. He starts to pray, "Oh, God, save me from this bear."

All of a sudden everything stops, in "freeze frame" style, and a voice booms from the sky, "Why should I? You've been blasphemous and denounced me all your life. You've told everyone who would listen that creation was an accident."

"You're right," says the atheist, "but at least make the bear a Christian."

The action resumed, and the bear fell to his knees, folded his paws and began to pray, "Lord, we are grateful for these gifts we are about to receive."

We gotta ask for the right things in the right way!

Treasure Mapping

Here's another powerful technique for reinforcing affirmations and bringing goals vividly to life. It's called treasure mapping. I can't recommend this tool too highly. Here's how to use it: Find a picture or visual representation of your goal and keep it in front of you. This way, you can visually see yourself owning the life changes you want, whether a material item, circumstance, virtue, or quality. At the most superficial level, it emotionalizes your goals and increases your desire to achieve them. At a much deeper level, it communicates to your subconscious mind and the power within you the seriousness of your goal and the importance of attaining it. Maybe you've done this or know people who have taped a picture of a new car, a slim body, or a trip to Paris on the refrigerator door. It unleashes the forces necessary to find creative solutions for overcoming both external and self-imposed obstacles that will quite naturally spring up when we set a big goal. (Remember Jack Boland's second force from our discussion on barriers?)

Treasure Mapping for a House

I experienced a dramatic personal example during my quest to achieve my goal of owning a training company. Our apartment was cheap and small and inconsistent with the image I had of myself as a successful businessman and provider for his wife and children. One day I ran into an old friend.

"How's it going, Byron?" he asked.

"Great, Matt. How's it going with you?"

"Really good," he said, "I've gone into real estate sales and I love it. Where are you living now?"

"We're renting a two bedroom duplex on St. Francis Street. It's pretty crowded but it will have to do for now."

"Well, here's my card. Let me know when you're ready to buy," he said.

"I don't think that will be anytime soon since I'm broke." "Oh," he laughed, "You'll be on your feet in no time." (I wished I had as much faith in myself as everyone else had).

We said goodbye and I went about my work and didn't think any more about Matt or buying a house, until he called a few weeks later, obviously excited. "I've got a house for you!" he enthused.

"But I still don't have any money." I said *un*enthusiastically.

"Don't worry about that right now, just meet me," he said, still bubbling. "I want to show you something special that is perfect for you."

I skeptically and reluctantly agreed to bring Patricia and meet him at the address he'd given me.

We pulled up in front of an attractive house in one of the nicest neighborhoods in town. It sat across from a peaceful, natural park filled with big, shady oak trees with a wide creek running through the center. In a word, it was perfect on the outside, and a tour of the inside confirmed it to be the house of our dreams. But we still didn't have any money, a fact I again pointed out to Matt, looking him right in the eye and speaking more slowly so I could make clear the part he didn't understand.

He smiled and said, "I know that. You've told me that three times," as though I were the slow one in this conversation. "But this'll work for you." He went on to explain, "I sold this house to these people less than a year ago, and now they have to move back to San Francisco. He's been offered the job of his dreams and he can't turn it down."

"I'm happy for him." I said dryly. "I still don't see how I'm involved."

Matt explained, "His wife and children are going to stay here until the kids finish school, and he doesn't want to have people traipsing through it while they are here alone. His asking price is reasonable. You'll have time to raise the down payment." He'd obviously put a lot of thought into this and had done a good job of selling himself on the whole deal.

"I don't know if I could have that much money by then. I'm working on straight commission and I don't have any guarantee," I objected weakly.

He was ready for that one. "I'll lend you the difference out of my commission!" he said triumphantly, closing the sale, knowing he had me.

There was no way I could pass up a deal like that, so I wrote a check for the deposit, emptying our checking account. Matt's car wasn't even out of sight before buyer's remorse kicked in and I started to worry. "What have I done?" I asked the heavens. "Where will I get the rest of the money in four months?"

Then I remembered the treasure map concept. I went to the title company and copied the title to the house. I crossed out the names of the current owners and printed my name and Patricia's in their places. I looked at that evidence of our ownership of our Vallombrosa home several times a day, letting the reality of owning the house sink deeply into my subconscious mind. I drove by the house several times a week and thought of it as our own. I pictured Michelle and Ana coming out the front door in the morning on their way to school. I imagined Patricia preparing dinner in the kitchen. I pictured myself backing out of the driveway to go to work.

The four months passed quickly and to this day I cannot recall exactly how I managed to accumulate the balance of the down payment.

Right-Brain Thinking

Now I know that when I repeatedly told Matt that I couldn't save that much money in such a short time, I was looking at my situation logically, using the left hemisphere of my brain, which could only draw upon what I'd done in the past. I actually made the money from sales commissions as a result of making twice as many sales in those four months. It was not a matter of luck. I'd found, in the right hemisphere of my brain, an extra dimension of creativity that enabled me to find the additional customers I needed and to be more persistent and more persuasive in selling to them. A critical part of the success of this technique is a strong desire, a vivid, emotional image of the goal with a physical picture or object, one you live with every day. I called it a miracle at the time but have come to take such things for granted now, using treasure mapping.

The Persian Prince

There once lived a king in ancient Persia who was wealthy beyond imagination, with servants to do his bidding and to make his life comfortable. Best of all, his only child, a handsome son who he loved more than all his possessions, gave him great joy. But the child was also a source of great sorrow for the king because the boy had been born disabled, with a misshapen body, and all the king's riches could do nothing to heal him.

On the morning of his fifth birthday, the prince came to his father and said, "For my birthday gift I would like a statue of myself in the garden so I can go out and look at it every day." He saw the pain in his father's eyes and quickly continued, "I don't want the statue to look like I am now, but the way I want to be when I'm grown and my body is strong and straight."

His father granted his wish. The statue was a beautiful, gold creation, designed by the master sculptor in the king's court.

Once it was finished, the prince spent hours in the garden looking at the statue. He stood between two trees and pushed his hands against them, strengthening his muscles. He swam in the river and ran through the kingdom for hours. He worked until he forced his atrophied muscles to respond and grow. His obsession with his physical development was so complete that a seeming miracle happened.

On the morning of his twenty-first birthday, he went to the garden and stood beside the statue. Looking out his window, the king saw two identical figures and could not tell which one was the statue and which was his son. The prince had become the person he'd dreamed of becoming!

And so can we!

Here then are some questions and actions for you:

Eighth Essential Tool: Affirmations

Questions and Actions

1. What are my strengths? Make a list of at least twenty-five of your personal strengths. Before you choose your affirmations, it is important that you build a base of self-confidence.

2. List any qualities that are missing from a description of your ideal self. Once you've identified your ideal self, the potential to achieve it lies within you. It only needs nurturing to be fully realized. You must be deadly serious about this whole process; it does not lend itself to lukewarm hoping. You've got to really want the success you describe.

3. Write your affirmations (eight to twelve should do it), then go back and ask yourself: Have I been too specific? While it's vital to be specific in goal setting, it would be limiting to affirm, too specifically, the conditions you want. For example, in my affirmations relative to the accumulation of wealth, I did not put down limiting dollar figures. I said, "an ever-increasing estate."

4. Read and visualize yourself as already being, doing, and having your affirmed object or condition.

5. Select one of your short-term goals and use the methods from *It Works* to achieve it. Here's the formula:

   • Write out your goal and read it aloud three times per day, morning, noon and night.

   • Think about the goal as often as possible throughout the day.

6. Select one goal and create a treasure map to implant it vividly in your mind.

Part Three

Skills for Success

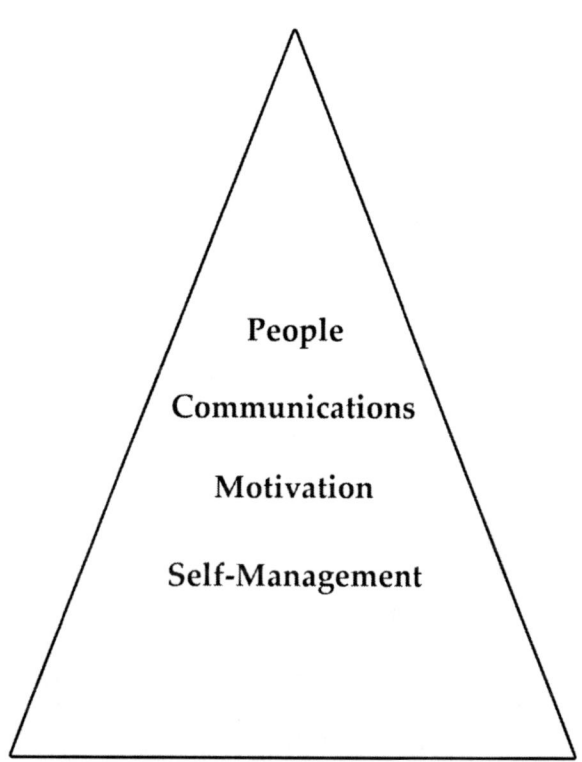

People

Communications

Motivation

Self-Management

The Ninth Essential Tool

People

"Every man is my superior in some way, and in that way I learn from him."

Ralph Waldo Emerson

I joined the several hundred people, milling around waiting for the start of a regional sales meeting at the Comstock Hotel in Las Vegas. I was scared, awkward, and felt out of place. My old nemesis fear was there beside me, whispering, "What are you doing? You don't have any business being here!" Everyone in the room appeared prosperous, confident, and successful. I surveyed the room, mentally preparing what I would say when I stood to introduce myself.

"Should I say something witty, or just be suave and let everybody see how cosmopolitan and urbane I am?" I wondered. "Maybe I should just mention that I'm an experienced old pro in the business and have been living abroad doing research the past few years," I mused to myself. I continued, "What a phony I am! Why can't I just be myself?" Nervousness and fear were scrambling around inside my head trying to protect me from my insecurities.

A Remarkable Man

Just then, a man I'd never seen before interrupted my inner ramblings. He looked at my name tag, stuck out a big, powerful hand and said with a friendly smile and a pronounced southwestern accent, "Mornin' Byron. Name's Lee Straughan."

I examined his leathery, weather-beaten face; it seemed better suited to someone working on a cattle ranch (which I learned later he had) than at a business meeting. He looked at me with a direct gaze and said, "You work with Boo Bue up there in San Francisco, right?" I figured he must be new, since I'd never heard of him before. Uncomfortable under his piercing gaze, I did what I always do under those circumstances: talk. I thought if I built myself up a little, I'd seem more important and overcome my nervousness.

"Yes, Boo's got a problem in his territory and asked me to straighten it out for him. I left a pretty high-paying job as a VP of an investment firm, but I've known Boo for years and I like him, so I agreed to do it." It wasn't all an exaggeration. I *had* left my job with an investment company; I'd gotten fired a month ago. And I *had* known Boo for a number of years and I *did* like him. And he *did* have a problem in the northern part of his territory—me. In other words, my story was reasonably correct.

Humor: The after-dinner speaker was grandly introduced by the master of ceremonies as "a man who made a million dollars in the oil business in the state of California." The speaker began, "Thank you for that fine introduction—it was reasonably correct. However, I'd like to amend a couple of things the master of ceremonies said. First of all, it was not the state of California; it was the state of Washington. And it wasn't the oil business; it was the timber business. And it wasn't a million dollars; it was a hundred thousand dollars. And it wasn't me; it was my brother.

And he didn't make it—he lost it!"

So I figured my reasonably correct introduction should impress this newcomer. "How about you?" I asked. "Are you a salesman over there in Albuquerque?"

"Sure am!" he said, "I own the franchise for New Mexico and west Texas."

Well, I'd just made a complete fool of myself. In all likelihood, Lee already knew my real story. However, he listened patiently, without judgment, as I blathered on. That's the way I remember our first meeting. This remarkable man became a trusted friend, a valuable teacher and advisor and made a tremendous impact on my career and my life.

Finding Heroes

There are people all around us who have the potential to serve as models or heroes and heroines, even as we are able to model for others. In five years we'll be the same people we are today, except for the people we meet and the books we read. Webster's New World Dictionary defines a hero/ine as: Any man or woman admired for his or her qualities or achievements and regarded as an ideal or model.

Lee Straughan is such a person; a successful investor and businessman, he best exemplifies the kind of hero I mean. Lee has spent countless hours serving others without personal gain. He taught me how to be the contributing human being I wanted to be. Lee is happiest when he uses his abundant gifts to help others; for years, he would fly around the country at his own expense to conduct training meetings for others in our business, to help us become more successful. At one meeting he gave us an idea that has proven extremely valuable to me. He suggested, "Carefully select some key people to assist you in attaining your goals."

Your Five Key Advisors

Lee said that every successful person needs several key professionals to assist him or her. Each profession or vocation may vary; you might select one or two different people depending on your unique needs. Here are the five Lee recommended for a small business owner:

1. Have a trusted banker who understands the unique nature of your business, is interested in you and your professional goals.

2. Select a good CPA, one who is willing to work with you as your business grows and to advise you.

3. A good insurance professional is necessary. Not being properly insured can wipe you out in the event of a disaster.

4. The right attorney will be your shield against all the things that can jump up to bite you in this litigious society in which we live.

5. And finally, you need a good financial advisor. As you start to earn money, you'll want to immediately start investing. Save and invest at least ten percent of all you earn. Don't wait until you can afford it because it is too easy to allow your standard of living to increase as your income increases.

An important point is this: There are multiple advantages to selecting these mentors, advisors and professionals. In addition to the support, encouragement, and professional advice they have to offer, you'll notice, as I did, a positive effect on your self-esteem.

Money

Let's step aside from our discussion of people for a moment to talk about this important subject of accumulating wealth. A book entitled, *The Richest Man in Babylon,* by George M. Clason influenced me. I always recommend it as a means to increase awareness and understanding of the process of becoming financially independent. Most people, including me, are concerned with accumulating an estate and being financially comfortable. Not having to worry about money frees us up to think about the larger, more important issues in our lives.

I have the advantage of being a product of the depression era, and as a result am motivated by the fear of not having enough money. I point this out because this may not be true for those of you born after World War II.

I recently had a conversation with Ethan Watters over lunch in San Francisco. Ethan, a Baby Boomer, is the author of *Urban Tribes* and he knows more than a little about the attitudes and values of his generation. He did a great deal of research for his book with members of his own "tribe" and others around the country. He recognizes that, for the most part, the fear of not having enough money does not motivate his generation; at least this was true for the groups he researched. They have never known psychological or financial insecurity. In my opinion this is not a bad thing; each generation will need it's own incentive to achieve a high degree of commitment to wealth accumulation.

Robert Kiyosaki, in the *Rich Dad, Poor Dad* series provides valuable financial guidelines for the present generation. Suze Orman is also a respected authority in this field, offering advice in her many books.

The following statistics, which I first read in my twenties in a pamphlet from Northwestern Life Insurance Company, gave me an incentive for saving and investing. Surprisingly, they haven't changed. Of one hundred people studied, from age twenty-five to sixty-five:

- One will be wealthy.
- Four will be financially comfortable.
- Five will still be working out of necessity.
- Thirty-three will be dead.
- Fifty-seven will be dependent on someone else for life's necessities.

When I read those statistics, I asked myself, "Where will I find myself on this list?" I hope that information is helpful to you, as it was to me.

The first step Clason suggests in the *Richest Man in Babylon* is to save at least ten percent of all you earn. I was broke and in debt at age thirty-eight, but once I formed the habit of this saving and investing practice, my net worth increased dramatically. I was delighted to observe how easy and rewarding it was. One does not have to earn a high income to benefit, and the sooner one starts, the easier it is. However, any time is better than never. The more important benefit I gained from this habit was increased self-confidence and self-respect.

As a reminder to my wife, I'd periodically say to her, "Someday the old Byron and Patricia will thank us for saving this money." We're not old yet, but we are already thanking those younger people we once were.

Evaluating Your Advisors

Now let's get back to the subject of people and Lee Straughan's list of five key advisors. If you are already advanced in your career, you can still benefit from his advice by using it as a checklist to evaluate those professionals you already have in place. If they're not in tune with your goals, you can take them to lunch and educate them. Tell them about your definite major purpose, hopes and goals. If they don't respond, are not interested, or don't understand, then you might consider finding a replacement.

My first attempts at finding my key advisors were less than satisfactory. The CPA was young and not as worldly as I wanted. The attorney I selected was of questionable honesty and was later disbarred. These were errors in judgments on my part; I hadn't taken the time to investigate them properly. Fortunately, none of my poor choices cost me money or reputation. When I moved to Portland, Oregon, to start my own training company, I started the selection process with a clean slate. Before selecting my new team of advisors, I asked for references, as Lee had suggested. Then I set about interviewing them to be sure they were someone with whom I'd be comfortable. I also felt it was important to find out if I was the kind of client they were looking for.

When I first attended Lee's training sessions, it seemed premature for me to find these people. I was just starting out; I was broke, had no fixed income and no financial reserve. At this point, I obviously did not feel like a very substantial businessman. But Lee said, "You don't know when, or to what degree you're going to need to call on these people for help." So even if you don't think you are ready for these advisors, it's not too early to select them.

Be prepared. It wasn't raining when Noah built the ark.

Think Big

As Lee predicted, these professionals became an informal, unpaid board of directors, advising me as I went along. The people I chose could see that I was serious about my business. There is one other benefit to assembling your team of professionals early. It has a dramatic and positive impact on your self-concept. I believe low self-esteem is the number one barrier to materializing our goals. Assembling a team of professionals forced me to think big, to think like a businessman, even when outside appearances didn't justify it. My desire to succeed and have everyone know it was so great that I'd stand up in meetings and introduce myself as "a company president trapped in the body of a salesman." The other salespeople in those meetings would laugh because I didn't seem to be a very likely candidate for business ownership.

Learn from Others

Another piece of good advice Lee gave us in his training meetings was to tap into other people's expertise. "If someone is scheduled to speak, who you believe will help you achieve your goals, go hear what he or she has to say. You don't have to agree with everything that person says." Jim Rohn, author and speaker, also expresses this well when he says, "Don't be a follower, be a student." There are two potential pitfalls we all face in our search for the truth:

- Blind acceptance of someone else's ideas because of his or her credentials.

- Our own arrogance, which creates a closed mind. The ego says, "I didn't think of that, so it's no good."

When you hear an idea that has worked for someone else, try it. Maybe it won't work for you, in which case you'll know from personal experience that it's not for you. Or possibly it will work better for you than it did for the person you heard it from. Then you are ahead of the game. This method will save you from having to learn everything by trial and error. Having a little humility will help you recognize that you don't have all the answers.

Humor: The village know-it-all walks into the blacksmith shop and starts nosing around, telling the blacksmith how to do his job. He picks up a hot horseshoe off the anvil, burns his hand and immediately drops it.

"Hot, isn't it." smirks the smitty.

"No!" cries the smart-aleck. "It jest' don' take me long to look at a horseshoe."

There are two ways we can find the speakers Lee advised us to hear:

- Check the local business calendar for the week, which lists the programs for the various clubs and associations for every profession.

- Find a club whose membership is made up of people with whom you want to associate. Join it. Select a committee that doesn't take a lot of time but gives you plenty of exposure so that you can meet the largest number of people you want to meet.

- Contact the office of an association in which you have a special interest. Join the group and network. A word of caution: networking is not prospecting or trying to make a sale. It's developing relationships that have the potential to be mutually beneficial. How do we develop those relationships? Become sincerely interested in others. Ask questions and listen. Resist talking about your business and yourself. People are far more interested in themselves than in others. Dale Carnegie wrote the classic best seller, *How to Win Friends and Influence People*, which has helped millions of people all over the world deal more effectively with others in all kinds of situations. It certainly helped me.

The Interview

By far, the all-time best method for learning from others is by interviewing them. It just makes sense to find out how accomplished, successful people in our field have achieved their success. It can be a rewarding experience.

One day, I attended a meeting of our local Rotary Club. I sat down in the last open seat, greeted the other members at the table and was introduced to a guest, Robert Pamplin, Sr., the former chairman of the board of Georgia Pacific. I said to Mr. Pamplin, "I've been an admirer of yours for some time. I speak to many youth groups each year and I believe they could benefit from your example. Would you grant me an interview so I could get your story first-hand?" He agreed.

After I left the meeting, fear set in. I said to myself, "What have you done? This man is a billionaire, on Forbes list of the wealthiest people in America. You don't have any right to take up his time." It took me a week to gather the courage to call him, yet when I did, he granted me an hour, and we ran a little long.

Throughout his career, Mr. Pamplin has been a leader and philanthropist. While with Georgia Pacific, he initiated the development of southern pine plywood, creating a whole new industry for the southern United States. Mr. Pamplin has a reputation for being a generous contributor. He said, "Make gifts while you're living. Enjoy seeing the benefits of your giving."

When I speak to groups and tell stories like those of Mr. Pamplin's, they benefit tremendously. These inspiring examples provide a model of the kind of positive, successful people we want to become. I also benefited because it expanded my self-concept— "I'm the kind of man who is comfortable interviewing community leaders." The important point here is that we can become more self-confident and make a contribution to our communities by being open to opportunities.

Dr. Don Ritchie, a highly respected dermatologist in California, gave me a great example of how another person can have a life-altering impact on you. Don said he felt it was his destiny to become a doctor but had became disheartened in school and was going to drop out after his first year of pre-med. Fortunately, a conversation with Jess, a friend and local businessman twenty-five years his senior, caused him to change his mind. When Jess heard about Don's discouragement, he took him aside and said, "Remember why you enrolled in medical school in the first place. You've always achieved everything you set out to do. Stick with it." This conversation dramatically reminded him of his purpose and his original reasons for choosing a medical career. It reinforced his belief in himself and his ability to achieve his goal. He went back to school, persevered, and pursued his goal to successful graduation. Think of the numbers of patients that have been helped by Don's caring, expert treatment. That wouldn't have happened if Jess had not taken the time to show an interest in Don at just the right time in the life of this young doctor-to-be.

Inspiring People are Everywhere

The big idea we've been discussing in this chapter is the role other people play in our development and success. An example took place in my life some years ago when Ana was involved in competitive swimming. I came home one day and my nine-year old angel said, "Dad, you know how you're always saying that we should spend more time together?"

"Yes," I said, feeling suspicious.

"And you remember how you're always saying you want to get in better shape?"

"Yes ..."

"Well," she said, "the Aqua Jets are forming an old person's team and if you joined it, you could drive me to practice so we could spend time together and you could swim and get in shape!"

That sounded good. (She was a good salesperson, even then.) The next morning we set out for swim practice. I was about forty years old and I met the other "old people" in the master's program: two twenty-one year olds at the low end, and a twenty-nine year old at the high end. Nonetheless, it was fun being with Ana and the exercise was helpful. After about a month Ana announced, "There's going to be a swim meet for the old people."

"Stop calling us the 'old people.' It's the Master's program," I said. "And I'm not going to be in any swim meet," I said firmly.

Two weeks later at seven in the morning we were in the car: Ana, four of her unbelievably enthusiastic teammates and me, headed for the swim meet a hundred miles away. The Aqua Jets and their Masters swimmers were competing against several other teams from around northern California. It was August and the temperature was over one hundred degrees. The "old people" didn't have a lot of swimmers so I had been entered in several events throughout the day, including the 400-yard freestyle. In mid-afternoon I said to myself, "I'm whipped. I've got to find a way out of this." But, there was no way out.

The Masters events were in the two outside lanes. I dove in and started to swim. Halfway down the pool I heard some shouting. I turned my head to breathe and there was Ana with her best friend, Verity Allen and a half-dozen more Aqua Jets walking alongside the pool yelling, "Go, Byron, Go! Go, Byron, Go!" These crazy kids were excited and pulling for me like my race mattered. Well, I couldn't let them down. I made the turn and they kept yelling, encouraging me and cheering me on. With each cheer I felt renewed energy and sense of commitment to our team. It's a good thing I was in the water: they couldn't see the tears that welled up in my eyes. Somehow I finished that race and had more energy coming out of the pool than I'd had all day. What an experience! I learned how powerful the support of team members could be. I've applied this lesson to the teams I've worked with, and to the company teams I've trained.

Correcting False Beliefs

I lived in Miami Beach as a young man, working as a pool attendant at a hotel. After my work was finished in the afternoon, I'd climb up on the diving board and practice various dives. I didn't really know how to dive but it was something I always wanted to do. I had failed trying to dive as a freshman in high school, and was convinced that I was not a diver. But one day I had an experience that shattered my negative self-image. I was blasted out of my erroneous beliefs about myself. Here's what happened:

I was doing my dives off the board when a man by the name of Art Lamore, a professional diver, strolled down the beach, stopped, and watched me for a while. As I was climbing out of the pool, he said, "You've got the makings of a great diver."

"What?" I couldn't believe he was talking to me! I'd admired his diving skill for some time, having watched him in a number of exhibitions.

He said, "You've got great balance and a good physique for a diver. Here, let me show you a couple of things."

He demonstrated a dive, and then had me do it. When I showed improvement, he was specific and enthusiastic in his praise. That encouraged me and I started to believe him. I listened eagerly to his suggestions for improvement. After he left, I stayed and practiced until it was too dark to see. The next day, I couldn't wait to get back on the board and practice some more! I could feel the improvement after that one lesson. Art showed up again that day; in fact he came almost every day and worked with me for about an hour. In three months, I was diving professionally in Sunday afternoon shows. I got paid twenty dollars for the show. Now, being a professional diver in Miami Beach at that time was like being an opera singer in Rome: everybody did it. But for me it was a significant event. Art's coaching corrected the false belief I'd been carrying around. It gave me self-confidence and a belief in myself as a person who was capable of changing. Since then, I've looked for coaches, mentors, heroes, and people from whom I can learn.

My recommendation to you is to seek out and draft people who will give you this kind of self-image-altering coaching, and listen to them.

The Master Mind Group

Here's another tool for working with people: Gather a group of people who share your values. Have regular meetings to explore ways in which you each might be able to achieve your goals and realize your purposes. Perhaps you could form a discussion group around the concepts in this book or any other book that embraces ideas you all have in common. You might consider brainstorming for solutions to problems that one or more members of the group are experiencing. Some people have referred to this exercise as mas-terminding. Whatever you call the group and the process, it does produce a synergistic result.

You can form the group from one of your already existing clubs or associations like a service club or church group. I'd suggest it not be overly formal, but do have an agenda with exact starting and ending times. People are time-starved more than ever today. Make sure you all agree on the components that will make it relevant and time well spent for everyone. Be sure it answers the question everybody has first and foremost in his or her minds: "What's in it for me?"

Your Most Important Person

Finally, the most important person in my life is my life part-ner, my wife. I have interviewed a great many people of impressive achievement and without exception, they mention another person in their lives as being an important contributor to their success: a spouse, significant other, friend, parent, or business partner. This is certainly true in my case. Patricia is my best friend, my confidante, and my business partner. This book is really our story. Her skills balanced my shortcomings; she backs me up and works alongside me. It would have been impossible to accomplish what we have without her. Partners such as these, who give more than they take, are critical to our success.

This chapter started with Emerson's profound thought. He rec-ognized the potential for learning in every other man and woman he met. That has certainly been my experience. All of the people mentioned in this chapter have taught me a needed lesson at a critical point in my life. Lee Straughan, Ethan Watters, those early professional advisors (good and bad), my present group of pro-fessional advisors, Boo Bue (again and again), Robert Pamplin, Ana and the Chico Aqua Jets, Art Lamore, and most importantly Patricia, my wife and best friend. I've heard that when the student is ready the teacher will appear. Each of these people and all of the others throughout this book have been models as I've ventured into new territories outside my comfort zone.

On Being a Hero

Mythologist Joseph Campbell helped me understand how we serve one another. "A hero ventures forth from the world of common day into a region of supernatural wonder; fabulous forces are encountered and a decisive victory is won; the hero comes back from this mysterious adventure with the power to bestow boons on his fellow man."

In our own heroic endeavor of creating a life worth living, all the while "enduring the slings and arrows of outrageous fortune," as Shakespeare said, we not only reap all of the rewards, but we come back with the power to benefit the rest of society. This may be the single most important reason for going to the effort of creating a memorable life. As we encounter these important people, these heroes in our lives, we must be sure to give to them the appreciation they deserve so they don't harbor any feelings of resentment toward us.

Humor: A couple married for sixty years were sitting in their living room one evening. Charlie, smoking his pipe and reading his paper, looked over at his wife. He thought about what a perfect mate she'd been, working alongside him through the good times and bad. He remembered how in those early years, when the going was really tough, she was somehow always able to put a good meal on the table. She was able, by sewing and mending, to make his clothes last. As he was thinking about her and how wonderful she was, he was struck with a sickening, stifling wave of remorse, because he couldn't remember once in those sixty years when he had ever given her any real appreciation. So with a tear in his eye he looked across the room and said, "I'm proud of you, Maud."

Now with the passing of over three quarters of a century, her hearing wasn't what it used to be, so she replied, "What'd you say, Paw?"

He cranked up the volume and repeated, "I said, I'm proud of you, Maud!"

She still couldn't understand him and said, irritably, "What'd you say, Paw? Speak up."

Now with a note of righteous indignation in his voice he shouted, *"I said I'm proud of you."*

She looked at him sadly and said, "Yes, I'm *tired* of you too."

Let's not put off telling any of these important people we've talked about in this chapter how much we appreciate them or how proud we are of them, and why.

Lets answer some questions and get into action.

Ninth Essential Tool: People

Questions and Actions

1. Select five people whom you admire. Make a list of their admirable qualities. Are these qualities you need to improve in yourself?

2. Select one of those people and arrange for an interview.

3. Who are your key advisors? Are they the right ones?

4. Select a team of support people: friends, associates, and like-minded people that you can meet with individually or in a group to discuss your goals and purpose. What can you do to help them?

5. List five things you can do to tell your partner or the number one person in your life that you value them most.

6. What one action will you take today to develop even more meaningful and mutually beneficial relationships?

The Tenth Essential Tool

Communication

"In the beginning was the Word."
—The Bible

Of all the elements influencing our success in life, words are perhaps the most important. We all know that the proper selection and use of vocabulary is our primary means of communicating with others, but we don't always recognize its effectiveness in our *internal* dialogue.

The purpose of this chapter is to increase our awareness of the words we select and the way in which we use them, in order to increase our odds of achieving success in our communications whether it is to ourself, another person, or a thousand.

We'll deal with some practical ways we can use words to increase our success and thus improve our world. Speaking, writing, and reading, along with non-verbal communication are the most important modes of sending and receiving information.

The Real Meaning of Communication

The word communicate is derived from the Latin *communicare*, which can be interpreted to mean: to share the same space, or, common ground. We share space with others with whom we have things in common, in our communities and when we commune with nature.

When we communicate, we share the same ideological, emotional, or spiritual space with others. In effect, we want another person to see the same picture we have in our mind and experience the same sensations we feel. That creates a joint domain. Talented writers transport us and affect our emotions and thoughts with their selection of words.

You and I have varying degrees of effectiveness and success in our day-to-day communications. This means we can control the quality of our environment and influence the attitudes and behaviors of others in a positive way. Let's talk first about the spoken word.

In earliest times, shamans used words in the form of stories to pass on tribal traditions and lore while sitting around a campfire. Six hundred years before the birth of Christ, in ancient Greece, Aesop told his fables so effectively that to this day children all over the world are able to grasp the deeper meanings of his seemingly simple stories and their morals. Jesus used parables to teach the multitudes who came to hear him preach.

Vernon Howard described the power and the profound impact of using properly told stories in his book, *Psycho-Pictography*. Howard demonstrates that an emotionalized picture, imprinted on the mind of the listener, has the potential to elevate that listener's concept of himself and his possibilities. Learning to communicate in this way will do more to help you achieve your dreams than anything else you can do.

The Power of Inspiration

Standing on the steps of the Lincoln Memorial in Washington, D.C. on August 28,1963, Dr. Martin Luther King Jr. spoke passionately to more than 250,000 civil rights advocates who had come from all across the nation to make their cause known. His brilliant selection of words, inspired by his spirit and vision, gave him an inner power that galvanized the civil rights movement, making him its definitive spokesperson.

The Power of Words

In Dr. King's example, we are talking about our use of words with others and the role they play in achieving success. Dr. King advanced his philosophy to the nation as he said, "I have a dream." In the process of doing this, he achieved two important objectives. He fulfilled one of the aims of modern philosophy, best expressed by the brilliant Spanish philosopher, Ignacio Gomez de Liano, author of *Illuminated Philosophies:* "… to strip off the armor of thoughts that have covered our way of seeing things." Gomez de Liano goes on to say, "We don't notice the extent to which words and word structures, that are ideologies, become prisons we can't get out of. To expand those confines is one of the ends of philosophy." Gomez de Liano's prisons have also been called paradigms or beliefs. The growth of the minority groups affected by the civil rights laws of the 1960s, moved from resignation to awareness.

Dr. King expanded the narrow confines of the consciousness of hundreds of thousands of Americans. He said, "The architects of our republic in the Constitution and the Declaration of Independence made us a promise. Their promise is a signed promissory note to which every American is full heir." In other words we don't have to subscribe to the beliefs that we've previously held. Dr. King gave inspiration to the people gathered that day by repeatedly saying, "I have a dream."

In *The Heart of a Champion,* Reverend Bob Richards said, "I believe a person is inspired when they see themselves, not as they are, but as they are capable of becoming."

Members of that loosely knit group of civil rights advocates became united with a common vision, and Dr. Martin Luther King, Jr. had the eloquence necessary to articulate that vision for them. Dr. King demonstrated how the careful selection of words, infused with spirit and vision, had the desired effect on his listeners.

If we don't select our words carefully, we run the risk of being misunderstood.

Humor: On the first day of school, the new teacher wanted to spell out the ground rules. "If you have to go to the bathroom, just raise your hand."

A boy in the front row said, "I don't see how that will help."

We must be aware of the importance of proper word selection and emphasis. The chairman of the Federal Reserve Bank in the United States is an example of someone who knows the importance of word selection and emphasis, because of the importance of American monetary policy worldwide. The men who have filled that position have historically been cautious in their use of language that could potentially invite panic or undue optimism.

The Lasting Impact of Words

We don't always fully appreciate the lasting impact our words can have on people. As an example, I was playing golf with Charlie Esler, a retired American banker living in Spain. As I told him about my business, he remembered participating in the Dale Carnegie Course early in his career.

He said, "My public speaking instructor said something that caused me to realize that I had the potential to be a good speaker. I told the class a story about a time I was pole vaulting in a high school track meet. I twisted when I came down and the spikes from one of my shoes punctured my hand!" Charlie was really excited as he relived the experience and even pointed to where the scar had been.

"When I finished talking the instructor said, 'Charlie, you are an exciting and effective speaker. You speak with emotion and intensity.' I've never forgotten those words. The confidence they gave me encouraged me to give a lot of talks and advance in my career."

The instructor's words helped Charlie see himself as one who could speak effectively and as a result, influenced the rest of his

life. We learned in the previous chapter the importance of influencing others. Charlie's experience gives us an example of the kind of
power and influence we can have on others with the proper selection of words, delivered with sincerity and feeling.

On the subject of public speaking: a large part of our effectiveness in our careers, service clubs, or community and church groups
will depend on our ability to communicate to groups.

Public Speaking

My recommendation is to do as Charlie Esler did— take a good
course in public speaking. From my experience, the twelve-week
Dale Carnegie Course in Effective Speaking and Human Relations
is the best one available. That will do more to accelerate your progress than anything else I know.

Training programs of that type assist us to be successful in our
communications. They help us use words properly and effectively.
They also help us understand our audiences and make it possible
for us to immediately get on the same page with our listeners.

Sometimes a question at the beginning will get us in step with
our listeners. But that does not necessarily guarantee that we'll be
in tune with our audience. We need to be sure we are clear.

Humor: The new Sunday-school teacher had heard that
starting his class with a question was a sure-fire way to begin. So he looked out at the group of six-year-olds and said,
"How many of you want to go to heaven? Raise your hand
if you do."

There were fourteen kids in the class and thirteen hands
went straight up in the air. One boy, the minister's son in
the front row, had his arms crossed and was frowning as he
stared at the teacher. "What's the matter, Johnny? Don't you
want to go to heaven when you die?"

"Oh, when I *die*," Johnny said, raising his hand, "I thought you were trying to get up a bus load to go this afternoon."

Getting in Step

Here's an example of the beginning of a presentation I gave a few years ago. The occasion was a recruiting meeting for Georgio Toscani, an Italian businessman who was building his management training company in Milan. He had invited a group of potential trainers to a meeting in an attempt to motivate them to join his organization.

"Buongiorno! Mi dispiace, non parlo Italiano. "(Good morning! I'm sorry, I don't speak Italian.)" So Georgio and Miranda must *traduccioni* (translate) for me when it's necessary.

"I come from a young country, a new country, only a little over two hundred years old. Yours is an old country, rich with tradition and history, respected by every other country in the world. You have given the world so many gifts in science, architecture, art, and music. We are richer because of Leonardo DaVinci, Michaelangelo, and all your great artists, from Caruso to Pavarotti. We even owe our existence to you, thanks to a courageous sailor born not too far from here in Genova, Christopher Columbus.

"Your country is going through changes. So is ours, and so is the rest of the world. Economies—governments—international commerce. We are no longer isolated from one another. What you do here in Italy affects everyone else in the world, as the day-to-day decisions of other countries affect you. These changes challenge us to adapt and do many things in different ways.

"But there is one thing that has not changed much in the last six thousand years of recorded history and that is our need to grow and develop as people, to live and work with one another. The need has never been greater for people to acquire the skills and attitudes for living in a rapidly changing world. Our gift from the United

States to Italy, to partially repay you for all you have given us, is in the form of a way to help people do this."

I went on to talk about the Dale Carnegie programs Giorgio would be offering and the benefits to the people they would be training. My purpose in that talk was to get action from that group of successful individuals. Giorgio called me the next day to say that all six of the possible candidates he had hoped to recruit had signed on.

There are four primary purposes for speaking to a group: to inform, to convince, to entertain, to get action.

I remember them with the acronym: **I C**an't **E**at **A**pples

To Inform—At a company or association meeting, we're sure to be asked to give a report concerning our department or committee. It's good to remind ourselves that reports can be deadly dull if they are mere recitations of facts. They should be treated with the same respect as any other important assignment.

To Convince—More and more, as we recognize the importance of building consensus in working with others, the need to get buy-in is critical. We must look at the present beliefs of our listeners and ask ourselves, "Why do they believe as they do?" "What would I need to understand about their beliefs?" The answers to these questions will help us do a more effective job of convincing them.

To Entertain—We might be asked to talk to a club or group about a trip, show slides, or perhaps to tell interesting stories at social functions. These are examples of speaking to entertain. Warning: We need to be very careful when telling jokes unless we are very good at it.

Humor: A criminal was sent to the penitentiary. The first night in his cell he heard someone at the other end of the cell block yell, "Number 32!" All the other prisoners started laughing. A few minutes later another prisoner called out, "Number 91!" Again everybody howled.

"What's that all about?" he asked his cellmate.

Wiping the tears of laughter from his eyes, the cellmate explained, "We've all been in here together for so long that we know each others jokes, so instead of telling the joke, we've numbered them all."

The new convict, wanting to fit in, waited until there was a lull then called out, "Number 16!" Dead silence. Nothing.

He turned to his cellmate and asked, "What happened? Wasn't that a good one? Nobody laughed."

"Oh yeah, that's one of the funniest," said his cellmate, "but you know how it is, some people just can't tell a joke."

If we are one of the ones who can't, we're better off leaving the joke telling to the pros until we've developed that skill or until we have something really unique to offer. To illustrate the value of uniqueness, here's another:

Humor: A couple months went by at the same penitentiary. The new convict, tired of being left out of the fun night after night, called out in desperation, "Number 122!" The house came down. Everybody roared, including his cellmate who was holding his sides, rolling on the floor. The new convict was amazed. "What happened?" he asked his cellmate.

"We've never heard that one before," his fellow con answered.

If we have a new one—or something original—we can still be entertaining. One way of doing this is to tell a story on yourself, a humorous incident about a time you did something and came out not looking so good. Audiences love the kinds of stories that demonstrate your humanness and humility.

Throughout this book I've used what I hope are humorous stories to illustrate or emphasize a point. I like to have fun, and when speakers are having fun and enjoying themselves, our listeners are too. I think that even when we have a serious message to deliver, as I intend this one to be, humor helps to lighten the delivery. The advantage of tying the message to humor, as opposed to just trying to be funny, is that even if the listener doesn't think the story is funny, he or she will still get the point.

To Get Action—Whether it is our responsibility to lead a fundraiser or blood drive, to make a sale or to persuade our children to do their homework, we need to employ this critical communication skill. If we always remind ourselves that people are interested in themselves first and foremost, we'll send the kind of message that is apt to get action most. If we tie our presentation to what *they* want, we'll get what *we* want. We must also persist and do as I've done in this book; repeat important points until we get the desired action.

Humor: The local church had been without a minister for some time, so the whole congregation was excited when they got the word that Reverend Jones had been hired. On his first Sunday, the church was packed and there was a feeling of anticipation in the air. When it came time for the sermon, they weren't disappointed. Preacher Jones got up and began his first sermon with, "I want to speak to you this morning about the imperative of girding your loins to meet the challenge of Christian living." Then he preached the kind of sermon they'd been wanting, and he did it with fire and passion. They all shook his hand, congratulated him and promised to see him next week.

The following Sunday there was an even bigger crowd, and they were early. When it came time for the sermon, the crowd leaned forward expectantly as Reverend Jones started to speak, "I'd like to talk to you this morning on the absolute necessity of girding your loins to meet the challenge of Christian living." He then proceeded to give the exact same sermon as the week before. The congregation was too polite to say anything; they just assumed he'd forgotten that he had already given that sermon.

The next Sunday, people settled in their pews and waited for the sermon. Reverend Jones looked out at them over his glasses and said, "This morning, I should like to address the important subject of girding your loins to meet the challenge of Christian living."

That was it; they couldn't take it any longer. One of the deacons in the back of the church stood up and said, "Reverend, you've already given us that sermon twice before! Don't you have any others?"

Reverend Jones replied, "Sure, I've got lots of them, but you haven't done anything about this one yet."

Reverend Jones was persistent!

Sincerity

This is a good place to remind ourselves that, in all things we say, we must be absolutely sincere and conduct ourselves with unswerving integrity in order to be credible with our listeners and have the self fit to live with.

Let's shift gears now, and talk about writing and reading.

Words Written

"What are you doing, Dad?" Michelle, my ten-year old daughter asked.

"I'm trying to write a book," I responded.

"How's it going?" she asked.

"I'm stuck. Nothing seems to be coming out."

"Well," she said, "sometimes you need to just write—get the words out of your head to make room for other stuff to get in."

I looked at her, amazed. She was always a precocious kid but I had no idea where she got that kind of wisdom. She was absolutely right. I was trying to operate both sides of my brain at the same time. The right side of my brain would come up with a creative idea, but before I could put it down on paper the left side of my brain would start to edit.

Let's look at some practical ways in which we can use the written word to increase our effectiveness. Reading and writing are our two most important modes of communication. Since that enlightening conversation with Michelle, I make a habit of getting the words out of my head and onto the paper to make room for new words and ideas.

Journaling

The best method for doing that is to keep a journal. I lived for years across from a park with a creek running through the middle. Frequently, I'd sit by the creek and let the ideas flow out of me. Sometimes I'd write profound philosophical observations, and other times I'd write pure drivel and usually it would be hard to tell them apart. Journaling is a way to communicate with ourselves. We're able to get half-formed ideas out of our heads and look at them on paper to see if they have value for us.

Subconscious Thoughts

Where do these half-formed thoughts come from? According to theorists, some come from the subconscious mind. Some years ago, when I participated in a personal development program, I was taught a technique for accessing the inner spirit. I was instructed to sit in a dim, candle-lit room at a table with a pen in my hand and a blank sheet of paper before me. Then, relaxed and with my eyes closed, allow ideas to develop on the paper without giving them any conscious thought. I was impressed with how well it worked so I know there is validity to the concept of subconscious communications. When he read the manuscript for this book, Bob James, the friend who first asked me the "what business are you in" question, commented, "I do this every week when I write my sermons."

Life Review Exercise

Another use for your journal is the Life Review exercise, which will reveal a goldmine of information. It enabled me to look at the experiences I'd had and the lessons I'd learned from them. I believe anyone will find it equally valuable as they set new goals for themselves.

Life Review Exercise Procedure

1. List all the places you've lived, in chronological order, starting with the place of your birth.

2. What were you doing in each of those places? Where did you go to school? Where did you work?

3. Who were the significant people in your life at each of those times and places? Parents or other relatives? Teachers? Mentors or advisors? Coaches? Pastor or Sunday school teacher? Friends? Boyfriend/girlfriend? Roommate? Co-worker?

4. What other activities were you involved in during those periods of your life? Athletics? Scouting? Music or drama? College? Camping? Partying? Raising a baby? Forming a band? Learning to drive a stick shift?

5. What memorable events occurred in your life at that time? Loss of a friend or loved one, from death, divorce, or mov-

ing away? An honor or achievement earned, academically, athletically or professionally? Especially meaningful trips or vacations?

6. What lesson or lessons did you learn from those events, experiences, and people? How do they influence your life now?

7. What character traits, attitudes, or behaviors do you see? Is there a pattern of repetition in similar experiences, at different times during your life?

Once you've completed the life review exercise and answered the questions, ask yourself, "How will this information help me to achieve my goals? What actions have helped me move toward achieving my goals? What distractions interfered with the person I aspire to be?"

This is the time to do some left-brain, or linear thinking and to examine our lives. As Plato suggested, "The unexamined life is not worth living."

Daily Review

Another exercise that can be helpful to us is a daily review of our actions. Spend a few minutes at the end of each day making two lists: "I'm Glad I Did," for the positive actions of the day and "I Wish I Had," for missed opportunities. This sort of regular meeting with ourselves, answering those questions, puts us in a position to weed out counter-productive attitudes and behaviors and to make better choices in the future. I would add here that we don't want to be overly critical of ourselves or conversely, become too proud. We are doing something that average people don't do: examining our lives to make changes. Roger Milliken of Milliken Textiles in Spartanburg, South Carolina, said in a speech, "The best definition of insanity I've ever heard is doing the same thing over and over again and expecting to get better results."

Notes of Appreciation

I recommend using another of my mentor's great ideas. Boo writes positive notes of encouragement, appreciation, recognition, and praise. He is a master of this thoughtful pastime. Not long but effective, always positive and specific, they have an impact on everyone who receives them. (I have a large folder of these notes—a thirty-year collection.) He is always alert for identifying those qualities he admires in others and tells them so. While waiting to catch a plane, for an appointment, in the air, or in a hotel, he'll dash off one of his famous notes and mail it from the nearest mailbox, not waiting until later when the idea and the feeling may have passed. We need to nurture our relationships with people; a written note of appreciation is one of the best ways to do it.

When we communicate with people in writing, we want to be sure that we do it appropriately: not too much and not too little. People are time-starved and we don't want to waste their time and possibly alienate them. Sometimes it's better to come directly to the point in our communications.

Humor: An ad in the personals section of the London Times: "Ninety-five-year-old man, smokes and drinks, desires to meet ninety-year-old woman who smokes and drinks. Object: smoking and drinking."

That's direct—perhaps a little *too* direct for effective customer relations.

A smoother, better example of superior communications is the way Michelle Thompson managed the customer service department of our company. She kept the benefits of the client's purchase at the conscious level by writing to them on a regular schedule. By looking at their situation from their point of view, she translated the benefits of our training programs into solutions to their problems. She made people feel included and they perceived, correctly, that she respected their time and didn't want to waste it. As a result of this professional approach, company sales increased.

Reading

Good literature is a great source of wisdom and knowledge, acquired by authors during the course of their lives, presented in compelling story form. The story can teach us an important lesson or provide us with perspective just when it is most needed. Indeed, you've noticed that I've relied heavily on stories to illustrate the key points in this book. Telling stories is a much better way to persuade people to take action than to threaten them.

Humor: Two mountain men meet on the road. Jeb takes out a jug of his homemade moonshine whiskey and says to Zeke, "Here, drink you some of this."

"No," says Zeke, "that stuff is awful."

Jeb lifts up his rifle and points it right at Zeke's head. "Drink it," he says.

Fearing for his life, Zeke takes a big gulp and, coughing and spitting, he hands the jug back.

Jeb hands him the rifle and says, "Now you hold the gun on me and make *me* drink."

As you can see, I've opted for the use of stories to get you to, "drink you some of this stuff."

Keeping abreast of the appropriate literature in my own field, I know what a challenge it is to stay current. It is demanding enough to find the time just to read about the changes and innovations that are taking place in most professions, much less look for historical precedents and references. Here are some solutions that can help us:

1. Prioritize our reading. What is really important?

2. Try the 30-10 system of reading. Schedule thirty minutes a day to read. Read aloud for ten of those minutes. This causes us to retain what we read more easily.

3. Reading in more detail than is necessary can be a time waster. I once thought I should finish every book I started. But that is not necessarily the best use of our time, especially when we read strictly for information. In *The 80/20 Principle,* an excellent book by Richard Koch, he suggests we increase our reading speed by reading the introduction, chapter one and the final chapter of a book first. Then we can decide if we want to go back and read more. His premise is that 80 percent of the value of the book can be found there; in reading those portions we'll learn the author's major points. (Note: if one had applied that technique to this book, they would have missed all the good stuff in this chapter.)

4. With time at such a premium today, more success-minded people are looking for ways to multi-task; to combine two or more activities to get more done. Audio books, for example are popular. I've listened to books on tapes in my car while driving. With an iPod you can jog, push the baby stroller, while listening to an audio book. Many people read while using exercise machines at the health club.

When I trained managers, executives, and other professionals over the years I frequently heard the objection, "I don't have time to read!" My answer to that is, "Did you watch television this week? If so, how much and of what quality?" Watching television is not inherently bad; we just need to recognize the difference between reading and watching television. The research on the difference between the two is overwhelming. Reading is active; it teaches and requires the brain to think. Television is passive; it requires no activity from the brain. The key question here, as always, is, "Will this move me closer to my goal?" A characteristic of the successful people I've encountered along the way was the breadth, depth and diversity of their knowledge, which contributes to living with balance and harmony. They are people who recognize the wisdom of Elbert Hubbard, who said, "The recipe for perpetual ignorance is to be satisfied with your knowledge and content with your education."

I found it useful to read books on business and management, sales and marketing, communications—and especially public speaking. I also have an interest in applied psychology, that is, the field of human relations. I benefit personally from studying finance and investing, health and fitness, philosophy, and religion and especially Zen Buddhism. I've enjoyed reading poetry over the years. These are all areas of interest for me; they might not be yours. Remember to adopt and adapt the ideas here to fit your own pursuits

One of the purposes of reading is to provide us with ideas to stimulate our thinking in order to take action. As Herbert Spencer, the great English educator and essayist, said, "The great aim of education is not knowledge, but action."

Now it's time for some questions and actions to put the above information to use:

Tenth Essential Tool: Communication

Questions and Actions

1. Do you keep a journal? If not, when will you start? Do you review your journal on a regular basis?

2. Practice the "I'm glad I did/ I wish I had" technique for at least one day.

3. Write at least three notes of appreciation: one personal, one work-related, and one other.

4. List three things you can do today to improve the effectiveness of your written communications, (perhaps an adult education course or a book on increasing your vocabulary).

5. Do you have a reading program? Select one book you feel would be most helpful to you right now. Commit to getting that book in the next three days. Make a plan to document your reading successes and extrapolate the important lessons learned from your reading.

6. How will you go about planning your next communication? Here's a suggestion for you. Look at all the business and social meetings you have scheduled for the next week. Plan your desired outcomes and strategies for achieving the objectives you've set for those meetings. Having objectives for your meetings is the behavior of a person who is living intentionally.

7. Do you have a plan for your communications this next week? Will they inform? Convince? Get action? Entertain?

Motivation

*Definition of motivation: that which causes
a person to act!*

Humor: Q: How many psychiatrists does it take to change a light bulb?

A: Only one, but the light bulb has to want to change.

The Power of Motivation

It was a little after midnight and I was driving down the I-5 freeway from Redding to Chico, feeling elated. At eleven o'clock I'd finished conducting a leadership training session. I was pleasantly tired; I'd been up since six that morning. My twenty-year old Mercedes hummed along. I had a ninety-minute drive home, and I was exhilarated from the mental, emotional and physical stimulation of the day. I loved my work.

The major cause of my euphoria however, was the promise of the day ahead. It was to be the day when I took the next giant step toward my major goal: owning my own training company. As a performance incentive, I needed to start a management training program in Chico with a minimum number of participants. It was to begin the day after tomorrow. Failure to do so would mean waiting another five or six months until I could qualify again.

I was one participant short to qualify, but I had the whole next day to sell and felt confident in my ability. I had four appointments, and there was no way I could fail. Just as I sat in my reverie, enjoying the anticipation of my success, disaster struck

The old Mercedes did the automotive death rattle; I just barely got it off the highway before it gave out and took its last gasp. I knew it was over. Big problem! I was in the middle of nowhere; there were no lights in sight and I had no cell phone. I remembered passing a truck stop a few miles back, so I had no choice but to start walking. I arrived at the truck stop an hour later and called the local AAA. The tow truck driver appeared a few minutes later to tow the car to the garage.

In the truck stop I asked every trucker in the place if he was headed south and if so, would he give me a ride. I told them my story and how important it was for me to get home. They all said they were sorry but it wasn't possible, as their company policy didn't allow passengers. I began to feel discouraged. It was getting late; I had to get home. I went back out on the highway and started hitchhiking. By now it was really late. The wind picked up and it was cold. I was on the verge of panic. No one stopped. I stood in the road and waved my arms, jumping back out of the way as the infrequent cars and trucks whizzed by.

Finally, at about four o'clock, a semi-truck pulled over and the passenger door opened. One of the drivers from the truck stop waved me in. "Get in quick," he said. I scrambled in and thanked him profusely. He said, "I'm not supposed to do this, but you look desperate. I can only take you to Orland." I fell asleep almost immediately and he shook me awake. "We're coming up to your exit," he said. "I'll just pull over and you jump out."

As the sun peeked over the horizon, I walked to an all-night diner with a taxi parked in front. The driver took me home; it was five-thirty. I was exhausted; I'd been up for almost twenty-four hours. I was famished and my first appointment was at seven o'clock that morning. I climbed in the shower, letting the hot water cascade over my aching body and giving myself a pep talk.

I was being tested to the max. It seemed as though, while all I wanted to do was crawl under the covers, I was being asked, "How sincere are you about wanting to be a success?" "I'm dead serious," I answered, resisting the temptation to lie down. I dressed, grabbed a bowl of cereal, jumped in my wife's car and headed for my first appointment. He didn't buy, nor did any of the others I talked to that day. At almost five in the afternoon, I was running out of time! My program was scheduled to start at one o'clock the next day and I was still one participant short. As I sat in the car on Main Street, going over my prospects, I thought of a possibility—a long shot—but a possibility. One of my clients owned an electronics store down the street. The program I was starting the next day was management training, perfect for him. He was a great guy but, by his own admission, his lack of organization was hurting his profitability. I went into the store; he was getting ready to close. "How's it going, Sandy?" I asked.

He was trying to find something on his cluttered desk and continued looking as he answered. "Same old stuff," he said. "Always behind and I'm not getting caught up."

"I'll bet that causes you a lot of stress, doesn't it?" I said.

He answered, "Too much. I've got high blood pressure and my doctor says I've got to slow down."

Now I was concerned for him. "Wow, that sounds serious," I said. "Why don't you slow down?"

"The business," he replied. "I really want the business to be successful and I'm afraid if I let up, it won't be."

"Suppose there was an immediate solution that would make things go more smoothly, reduce your stress and increase your bottom line. Would that be something you'd want to know about?" I asked.

He stopped searching for the missing paper: I had his full and undivided attention. "What do you mean?" he asked.

"Look at this," I said and went through the management areas covered in the six-week program, relating each of them to my personal knowledge of him. I pointed out how his business would benefit by eliminating some of his counter-productive practices. He became very interested and agreed that it was just what he needed, but resisted starting the next day. We talked more and he finally said, "Let's do it." He wrote a check and I walked out of his store at seven o'clock.

By now it had been thirty-six hours since I'd slept, but I was happy and relieved; I'd almost missed my goal. I fell into bed, exhausted.

I met Boo at the airport the next morning with the good news. We prepared for the session and had an early lunch, talking excitedly about my success. By twelve-fifteen the participants started arriving. By twelve forty-five they were all there, with one exception—Sandy. I waited another five minutes and called him.

He answered and said, "I can't do it, man. I've got a supplier salesman here now, and my clerk didn't show this morning. I'm here by myself."

I hung up and told Boo to start at one o'clock, on schedule. I had to go get Sandy. I rushed to his store, and sure enough, he was talking to a salesman and he was all by himself. I interrupted their conversation.

"Do you want Sandy to do a better job for you?" I asked the vendor.

"Yes!"

"Do you think he needs to be a better manager?"

"Absolutely!" He said.

I could tell he'd been dealing with Sandy for some time and was distressed with his lack of organization.

"Then can you see him on your way back south, after you go to Redding?"

"Yeah, I could. Why?"

I told him about the management program and I described the ways Sandy would benefit and what it would mean in terms of increased sales of the vendor's product.

He said, "I'm all for it!"

"What about my clerk?" Sandy asked.

"What's her phone number?" He gave it to me and I called her. "What would it mean to you if your boss were able to operate like a sane man for a change?"

She said, "I'd love it!"

I told her the situation very quickly and said, "Will you come to work right now?"

She must have sensed my anxiety because in less than twenty minutes she walked in the door. I hurried Sandy out to my car (I wasn't going to take any chances), and we walked into the room at one-thirty. In no time, he was hooked. He liked what he heard as I knew he would.

At the end of the afternoon, as everyone was leaving, he shook my hand and thanked me. "This is just what I need. I'll see you next week."

When everyone had left the room, Boo said, "Congratulations, Mr. Territory Manager!" The look on Boo's face and his congratulations felt almost as good as the realization that I had, against great odds, achieved my goal!

Strong Desire

Why have I told you this story? Because I believe that it demonstrates the most important lesson in motivation. That is: even when all the negative circumstances in the world conspire to shatter our dreams, if our desire is strong enough, we'll find a way to achieve those goals.

Perhaps you've heard the story of the young boy who asked the village wise man, "How can I be successful in life?"

The old man said, "Come with me." He took the young boy by the hand and they walked down to the bank of the river. Instead of stopping, the old man kept walking until the water was over the boy's head. The old man held on to his hand tightly. The boy struggled, and just when it seemed as though his lungs would burst, the wise man pulled him to the surface. The boy crawled up the riverbank on all fours, gasping for breath. Then the wise man spoke. "Just now, when you were under the water, what did you want?"

"Air," gasped the youth. "All I wanted was air!"

"When you want success as badly as you just wanted air, you'll have it."

The Source of Desire

Where does our deep desire for personal success come from, and how do we keep it alive? That desire lies deep within each of us. That's why I've continually stressed thinking, introspection, and self-analysis throughout this book. One's dreams are individual and personal, so each of us has to find them for ourselves. As Socrates said, "Know thyself."

It seems that we must all have an internal cost/benefit weighing device that is constantly in action, asking us, "Is the choice I'm faced with right now more apt to supply me with pain or pleasure? Is the effort required to take this action worth the reward?"

Our motivations explain why we have or have not achieved desired results in our lives, so far. Most of us would like to have better results in some areas of our lives, but we're not motivated enough. Maybe you've heard the expression, "Everybody wants to go to heaven but nobody wants to die." This point goes to the heart of the issue. We would all like to have or achieve things in our lives, but in too many instances we aren't willing to pay the price.

Humor: In the Ozarks, one old-timer stops by to visit another old-timer settin' in a rockin' chair on his porch. As they're talkin,' the owner's dog is a-layin' next to him, moanin' softly.

"What's wrong with yer dawg?" drawls the visitor.

"He's settin' on a nail," says the dog's owner.

"Well, why don't he move hisself?" the friend wants to know.

"It don't hurt him enuff yet," says the owner.

Don't Accept Mediocrity

At the beginning of this book, I identified myself as Walt Whitman's "average man in average circumstances." I've experienced setbacks and have found myself more than once in distressing circumstances. But I also knew that I didn't want to remain average, which was especially problematic for me when, at thirty-eight, I returned from Spain dead broke. There was a disparity between my philosophy of success, which I had been teaching and preaching all my life, and the circumstances in which I found myself. That incongruity was an important factor in my motivation to excel. My biggest fear was that I would end up having lived a mediocre, average life. (Average is defined as the worst of the best or the best of the worst). I thought about what Dr. Jennings said in that talk in Scottsdale, Arizona, just a few years before: "There is nothing sadder than for a person, upon reaching the age of retirement, to look in the mirror and realize they'd settled for less than their best." I thought, even if I get a good job and do well, if it didn't challenge me fully, I wouldn't really be satisfied. I also realized that I was the ultimate judge of whether I'd succeeded or not. I found this poem, which helped me and I believe it will help you.

The Guy in the Glass

When you get what you want in your struggle for self
And the world makes you king for a day,
Just go to the mirror and look at yourself,
And see what that guy has to say.

For it isn't your father or mother or wife
Upon whose judgment you must pass.
The fellow whose verdict counts most in your life
Is the one staring back from the glass.

You may be like Jack Horner and chisel a plum,
And think you're a wonderful guy.
But the guy in the glass says you're only a bum
If you can't look him straight in the eye.

He's the fellow to please—never mind all the rest,
For he's with you clear to the end.
And you've passed your most dangerous, difficult test
If the guy in the glass is your friend.

You may fool the whole world down the pathway of years
And get pats on the back as you pass.
But your final reward will be heartache and tears
If you cheated the guy in the glass.

Dale Wimbrow

Circumstances

I put pressure on myself to overcome the inconsistency of what I dreamed of being and the reality of my circumstances. But I remembered George Bernard Shaw's saying, "I don't believe in circumstances. If I don't find the circumstances I want, I create them."

In other words, I created the distressing set of circumstances in which I found myself and I had it within my power to change those circumstances. We all have this power.

Positive Domain

If we have reached a point in life where we are progressively realizing—working toward but not yet attained—what we define as a worthwhile ideal or goal, we are in the positive domain. We are being the very best we can be. Our only other choices are neutral or negative.

This positive domain is characterized by being optimistic, upbeat, enthusiastic, and creative. The world is alive, colors are vivid, and sounds are melodic and pleasing to our ears.

The negative domain is made up of depression, dullness, and a lack of desire to do anything: a general avoidance of life. Sights and odors of all kinds seem to offend; sounds are discordant.

Between these two extremes is the neutral domain, in which we are neither positive nor negative; in some respects the worst condition of all. It is characterized by feeling emotionless—no ups or downs. The blahs. Everything seems gray and monotone. There are no contrasts in our environment. We are not stimulated by anything.

Andrew Carnegie aptly described these contrasting conditions when he said, "Money will not make you happy; it will merely keep you from being unhappy." In other words, escaping the negative domain will only take us into the neutral domain, which will not make us happy. Most popular magazines promise, in articles and advertisements, an escape from the negative. But the latest prescription drug, new car, new house, or new relationship will not make us happy. The optimum state for human beings who are motivated in a healthy way is one in which we experience life fully and are, as a result, being the best possible people we can be: serving our families, our companies, and our communities. We enter this optimum state when we are pursuing what *we* consider to be a worthwhile goal.

Our Higher Responsibility

It is in this state, too, that we become most aware of our power and our responsibility to serve at a higher level, to make a difference in the world. This is the influence that draws us to devote time, energy, and money to service, spiritual work, or humanitarian organizations. At its most advanced level, it causes us to ask ourselves, "How can I make a difference and make the world a better place?" When fear rears it's ugly head, we can counter it by reminding ourselves of our power and draw inspiration from the words of Marianne Williamson in *A Return To Love,*

> Our deepest fear is not that we are inadequate. Our deepest fear is that we are powerful beyond measure.
> It is our light, not our darkness, that most frightens us.
> We ask our self, who am I to be brilliant, gorgeous, talented and fabulous?
> Actually, who are you NOT to be?
> Your playing small doesn't serve the world.
> You are a child of God.
> There's nothing enlightened about shrinking so that other people won't feel insecure around you.
> We were born to make manifest the glory of God that is within us.
> It is not just in some of us, it is in everyone. And as we let our own light shine, we unconsciously give other people permission to do the same.
> As we are liberated from our own fear, our presence automatically liberates others.

Ms. Williamson's words are also reminders that the rewards of success are accompanied by the responsibility of success.

Four Skills for Success

So far, we've talked about self-motivation, an important aspect of understanding ourselves in our pursuit of success. From this awareness of ourselves, we can understand the motivations of others. When we think of success, it is valuable to recognize the four skills or pathways that contribute to its achievement:

1. The intelligent application of our own best skills and talents; our trade, craft, or area of expertise. (Hands work)

2. The regular, prudent investment of a portion of our earnings to develop an estate. (Money works)

3. The most valuable of the four, the disciplined use of our mental resources to creatively find solutions to problems and to expand our possibilities. (Ideas work)

4. Recognizing and using the talents of others. (Others work)

Of these, leadership, the ability to produce results through others, is clearly the most challenging because everyone places his or her own interests as their priority. This is an important and separate skill and deserves significant time and study. When jobs are scarce and people are not as psychologically secure, they can be motivated by fear and threats, which only works as long as they feel threatened.

Humor: A drunken cowboy staggers out of a saloon just in time to see an old prospector tying up his mule in front. "Hey, old-timer," he yells, "can you dance?"

"No," says the prospector. "I never learned how to dance."

"Well, you better learn," laughs the cowboy as he pulls out his six-shooter and starts firing at the old man's feet.

The prospector is certainly motivated but he's also counting, and when the sixth shot is fired he stops dancing. His motivation is gone, and he decides to do some motivating of his own. He reaches across the mule and pulls a long rifle off his saddle.

"Hey, cowboy, did you ever kiss the back end of a mule?"

"No," says the cowboy in a shaky voice. "But I always wanted to."

What Motivates People?

If we are going to effectively use the talents of others to produce results, we'd better know something about what motivates them.

Individuals' interests are unique and differ according to circumstance. If we are to use the highest and best skills of others to achieve our dreams, we must help them achieve theirs. That implies we know what that unique individual's dreams are at this time in his or her life. We know from the work of Abraham Maslow that human beings have an expanding series of needs. Each one of these needs will only motivate an individual until he or she is satisfied, then it is replaced with a higher need.

The Perception Portrait

One approach to understanding a person and pinpointing where he or she is in the hierarchy at any given time is to draw a perception portrait. That is, through organized questioning, find out how he or she sees the world: past, present, and future, and what his or her goals are. This was very effectively accomplished at Stanford University when John Ralston was the head football coach there. He and his assistants met with every player on the team, de-

veloping a perception portrait of each one of them. As Ralston explained, Stanford's football players were in school for an education
first and to play football second. The coaches had to know "how
much football they had in them" at any given time during their
career. Did that information help the coaches? Apparently it did;
they won the Rose Bowl two years in a row. Obviously that was
not the only thing that contributed to their success but the players
were motivated, in part, by the genuine interest Ralston and his
assistants expressed in them. You can adopt and adapt this idea
to your own life and career with anyone with whom you are in a
relationship.

When drawing a perception portrait, start with the present. Get
a clear image of how the person you are interviewing sees their
present situation: job, family, home, social life, etc. Don't write the
answers down. Let each question be determined by the answer to
the previous question. Make mental notes. Two important points
here: this is not an interrogation or the third degree. It should be a
give and take; let them know some things about you, too, but limit
the amount of time you spend taking about yourself.

Also, your intention here is to send the message that, "Since
we're working together, I'd like to get to know you better."

Next, find out how that person sees the world in the past. Where
did they work before? Grow up? Go to school? What was it like for
them growing up? What size family did they come from? Where
did they fit in the birth order? How has the person they are today
been influenced by their earlier life? This information makes it far
easier to understand why a person behaves as they do, and enables
us to empathize with them by noticing ways in which the two of
you are alike and have had common experiences.

The third general area is to draw the perception portrait in the
future. What would their ideal future look like in five to ten years?
What do they expect to happen? What would the interviewee like

to have happen? What would they like to be remembered for? What would they like to achieve?

This method of getting to know the important people in your life can enrich your relationships and be advantageous to both of you, as you live and work together. Now let's put the information from this chapter to work.

Here are some questions for you and some actions for you take:

Eleventh Essential Tool: Motivation

Questions and Actions

1. Recall a time when you persevered to achieve a goal. What were the details of the experience? Who was involved? Where did it take place?

2. What qualities or strengths did you demonstrate in the process of achievement? What did that experience teach you about your motivation?

3. Select a goal that requires extra self-motivation. Make a list of benefits you'll derive from achieving that goal. Do the same with your other goals. Make a treasure map and write affirmations that you can use to fan the flames of your desire!

4. List the reminders you can give yourself on a regular basis to stay focused on your goals.

5. Based on what you've learned about yourself in this chapter, what one action will you take to achieve that goal? When will you take it?

6. Select a person — family member, co-worker, or employee— that you can help to achieve one of their goals. Use the Perception Portrait to find out what they want and why they want it? Make notes. Select the method that is most apt to motivate them to achieve that goal. What did you discover about motivation as a result of this exercise?

The Twelfth Essential Tool

Self-Management

"If all we ever do are those things which are convenient and comfortable, the great things in life will never get done."
—George Bernard Shaw

Taking Responsibility

"You're fired." Marty said, not unkindly.

I liked the man who had just become my former employer with that forthright pronouncement. He never wasted time, as I tended to do, by searching for an indirect way of saying what he meant to avoid hurt feelings. The fact that I didn't like the job and was no good at it took some of the sting out of my unceremonious dismissal.

I'd been back from Spain less than six months and was still trying to get back on my feet financially. I must confess, my first thought was not, "Wow, how is this company going to survive without my skill." No, I was more concerned with the nice paycheck I'd been receiving while trying to figure out how I could get into the business of helping other people grow. In fairness to Marty and the other officers, they gave me every opportunity to realize that ambition with them. We just had dramatically different styles.

The best thing I ever did was to ask Marty, "What do I need to do on my next job to perform satisfactorily?"

He said, "Dot your i's and cross your t's. You need to pay attention to details."

I thanked him, walked out of his office and picked up my severance check.

On the long drive home I rehearsed my explanation to my family about Marty's judgment in letting me go. I also had a chance to think about what he'd said about my i's and t's. Being honest with myself, I had to admit that I didn't always listen and was definitely lacking attention to detail.

As I looked more deeply and honestly at myself, I realized that in addition to not "dotting my i's and crossing my t's," there were other impediments to my success; this was symptomatic of a much more serious problem. There were many other little things that related to the same issue.

In retrospect, it sounds as though I arrived at these discoveries all at once; this is not the case. They became clear over a period of time, as a result of meditation, reflection, keeping a journal, and participating in training programs designed to increase my awareness.

Helpful Insights

Two insights were most helpful to me:

- I, along with most everyone else, will go to great lengths to avoid being uncomfortable and doing things I don't like to do.

- My view of reality was seriously flawed. I tended to look at the world not as it was, but as I wished it were.

Self-Discipline Reminders

I dealt with the first of these issues by focusing on my purpose and keeping my major goal in the forefront of my consciousness. That helped me make choices that contributed to fulfilling that purpose and attaining that goal.

"Successful people form the habit of doing the things

failures don't like to do. Successful people are influenced by the desire for pleasing results. Failures are influenced by the desire for pleasing methods." *The Common Denominator of Success,* Albert E.N. Gray

"The chief cause of failure and unhappiness is trading what we want most for what we want at the moment." Source unknown

"If it's your job to eat a frog, it's best to do it first thing in the morning. And if it's your job to eat two frogs, it's best to eat the biggest one first." Mark Twain

These quotations were useful reminders, keeping me on track as I moved toward my goals. They reminded me to prioritize my shortcomings, to work on the one that was my biggest impediment first and to get started on it right away.

Beliefs

It took much more observation and analysis to understand my view of the world in light of the second issue. A scene from one of my favorite movies illustrates my conclusions: "You either get busy living or you get busy dying," Andy said to Red in *The Shawshank Redemption.* The movie was about the deliberate dehumanization of men in the fictional Shawshank Prison. Its success in institutionalizing, or breaking the prisoners was dramatized by the suicide of a parolee who found he could not live on the outside. Red was ready to surrender to that same mentality. However, he was inspired not to succumb as he watched his friend, Andy, who didn't and wouldn't surrender. Andy managed to retain his identity and hope of freedom, and achieved it after 20 years.

I've listened to countless people in my training sessions over the years report on their own self-imposed limitations and the frustration they felt by being incarcerated in imaginary prisons of their own making.

We're all faced with the same kinds of potentially limiting conditions, created by our beliefs. Conditioning creates the limiting environment a fish experiences in water. The fish has never known, and in all probability cannot conceive of any reality other than water, but almost certainly, instinctively knows that it would die out of that environment.

The difference between a fish and a human being is that if we have the courage to extricate ourselves from our environment, we do not suffocate but enjoy a new freedom and an expanded sense of self.

Mental Entrapment

I became aware that I, too, was following the crowd and was subject to the same influences as everyone else. I was unconscious and not deliberate in my actions. Earl Nightingale, described this unconscious behavior as, "following the follower."

I discovered a valuable technique for extricating myself from the counter-productive influence of going along with the crowd and eliminating the impediments that were standing in the way of my success.

A Recipe for Self Improvement

The American statesman and inventor, Benjamin Franklin, deserves credit for the idea. In his autobiography, he details his plan for self-improvement.

Franklin selected thirteen areas in which he felt a need to improve. Then he systematically worked on improving himself in each area for one week, keeping careful records of his progress. Why thirteen? Because he worked on each area for one week at a time, and completed four cycles each year. Franklin's autobiography is fascinating reading for any serious student of success. His

successes and means of achieving them are inspiring and instruc-
tive.

Thirteen Areas

If a person wants to adopt this approach, how should he or
she go about selecting thirteen proper areas for self-improvement?
For me, the answer was right in front of my eyes. My affirmations
represented the areas in which I most needed improvement. I had
been visualizing myself as perfect in those areas. Now I needed to
add measurements to those affirmations in order to turn them into
goals. Measurements would tell me that I'd made progress in that
area.

My affirmations were the natural areas of self-development. If
a person feels there is value in taking a systematic approach to self-
improvement, this method will accelerate his or her progress.

Thirteen Areas of Self-Improvement:

Choice	Planning
Business	Responsibility
Fitness	Community
Discipline	Family
Mental	Organization
Finances	Goals
Spiritual	

This self-improvement technique of one area per week sup-
plies an organized, systematic method for developing new habits.
It is easiest to adopt for people who are linear thinkers—left- brain
types—because it is so structured.

It is for that very reason, however, that it is valuable for right
brain, creative types. It forces a discipline on us that we need. Ralph
Waldo Emerson said, "What we all most need is someone to make
us do what we know we ought to do." Here we're substituting a

structure of our own design to make us do what we know we ought to.

The Motivating Force

Brian Marsh described a wonderful example. During a period in his life he was seriously overweight and, began to experience major health problems as a result. He went to a doctor who told him he couldn't be treated until he lost one hundred pounds, and that if he didn't lose weight he wasn't going to make it (doctor-speak for "You're going to die.") His doctor recommended a dietitian who said, "Here's a regimen for you to follow. You must do exactly what I tell you to do, or I won't work with you. If by next week you haven't lost at least two pounds, don't come back." There it was.

Brian had the motivation, (do or die), and the system (the diet and exercise program) he needed. He stuck to the diet and the walking program and even added a few flights of stairs on his own accord. In eleven months, he exceeded his goal and lost 105 pounds. This story is a great example of what can happen if we have a purpose, a goal and a system.

Coach John Ralston has his own weight management system. Ralston steps on the bathroom scale every morning to monitor his weight. If he is so much as one pound over his ideal weight, he fasts for the day. What an example of daily self-management! What discipline!

I remember another example from one of my teachers when I was seven or eight years old. The teacher said, "To develop self-discipline, buy a Hershey's candy bar and eat just one square each day." I've never tried this so I'll leave it to some one else to test it.

It was always so difficult for me to improve in the area of self-management; I was a slow learner and sometimes thought I'd never learn.

Humor: A guy looking for a vacation answered an ad in a San Francisco newspaper for a round trip cruise to Mexico. All expenses included for one hundred dollars. Heck of a deal! How could he go wrong?

He called the number and was told to show up, ready to go, at two o'clock in the morning on Pier 33. He showed up at the appointed hour. It was pitch black. Suddenly, he felt a stinging blow to the back of his head. He woke up a couple of hours later shackled to an oar on a huge ship, rowing like a galley slave along with a hundred other "vacationers," who had answered the same ad. He realized he and all of his shipmates had been shanghaied. He turned to the guy next to him and said, "I wonder if they'll at least feed us some gruel."

"I don't think so," his fellow passenger answered. "They didn't last year."

Some people are really slow learners!

Choices

Positive, healthy choices lead us toward the attainment of our goals.

An old song said you have to "accentuate the positive, eliminate the negative." In the area of self-management, we have an ideal opportunity to incorporate choice into our daily lives. If we just make small, bite-size, minute-to-minute, positive choices, we can progress rapidly in a surprisingly short period of time. Why not record daily choices in a journal and review them at the end of the week? It's a way to build self-esteem.

Choice! I've referred to this repeatedly:

- We choose our purpose; more accurately, it chooses us.

- We choose our values: the person I want to be.

- We choose our thoughts, filtering out counter-productive influences; programming our subconscious mind, thinking positive thoughts using affirmations and treasure mapping.

- We choose our future by setting goals, creating and following plans of action to attain them.

- We choose our actions by asking ourselves the key self-management question: "Is what I'm doing now moving me closer to my goal?"

Twelfth Essential Tool: Self Management

Question and Actions

1. Where do you currently demonstrate self-discipline in your life? Make a list of the many things you already do on a regular basis that are inconvenient and uncomfortable. Things like exercising, walking your dog in bad weather, or studying instead of watching television.

2. List some of the important areas of your life in which you need to exercise more self-discipline.

3. How can your affirmations serve as a template to design a regular program of self-discipline?

4. Plan some small actions you can start with, for example, something as simple as eating an apple. As the old saying goes, "An apple a day keeps the doctor away." Many of us are not even self-directed enough to do that! This might be a start for us.

5. Ask five people you admire how they discipline themselves. Ask yourself, "Can I adopt that for myself?"

6. Adopt Ben Franklin's thirteen areas for self-improvement plan and implement it.

Part Four

Putting It All Together

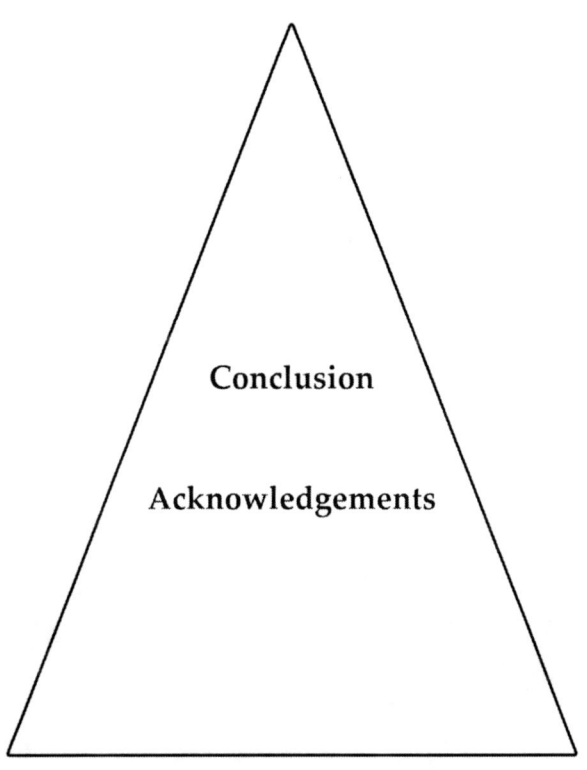

Conclusion

Lord, we ain't what we ought to be.
And, Lord, we ain't what we wanna' be.
And we promises you, Lord,
We ain't what we're gonna' be.
But we wanna' thank you, Lord,
We ain't what we use'ta be!
　　　　　　　　　　　—Old Southern preacher's prayer

That old preacher expressed it well. There is more work to be done, but see what we've already achieved! If you've read this book, answered the questions, and put each of the tools to work, attitudinally you are a new person, headed toward an even more exciting life. You won't let yourself settle for being less than you can be. At this point we can clearly recognize the wisdom of University of Pennsylvania psychologist, Martin Seligman's statement: "Human beings want to have meaning. They want to *not* wake up in the morning with a gnawing realization that they are fidgeting until they die."

Yes, we have grown and changed since we started reading this book, and there is so much more to do. However, let's appreciate the progress we've made and recommit to our future. (I'm still committed to helping the maximum number of people achieve their full potential.) I wrote this book because I still have the desire to serve.

Why This Book Will Work for You

Jayme's Story

Jayme Westrom, a high-energy, fun, twenty-six-year-old friend, brought us up to date on what was happening in her life.

"My full-time job for the past three years has been teaching at a Montessori School in Baltimore. I'm also enrolled in night school in a graduate program to get my master's degree in teaching, and I'm taking flying lessons to get my private pilot's license. To make extra money, I have a part time job building models for an architectural firm."

With that schedule, it was easy to see that she needed a break, "But," she went on, "I'm really starting to question what I want to do with my life. I don't know if I'm doing what I want to do for the rest of my life"

"I think it's good that you are asking those questions now, Jayme," I said. "I've heard too many stories of people who spent their whole careers climbing the ladder of success only to find, too late, that the ladder was leaning against the wrong wall. As a result, they were disappointed, frustrated, and unhappy. They found themselves in mid life with the terrible gnawing feeling of unmet expectations and frequently have a so-called mid-life crisis."

"Why do you think that happens?" she asked.

"In too many cases, they didn't ask the questions you're asking now until they spent too much of their lives trying to conform to other people's ideas of what they should do with their lives, or they just never stopped to ask themselves what they really wanted."

"I hope that doesn't happen to me," she said.

"I don't think it will," I said. "You're intelligent and self-directed, and besides, a person can make changes and improve the quality of their life at any point. In fact, I'm writing a book on that subject right now. I believe anyone can create a really satisfying, successful life for themselves."

"Really?" That sounds like something that would help me—could I read it?"

Of course I said yes.

A month later, I received this email from Jayme: " I have a new plan for my future, which is largely due to reading your book. The business I'm in is teaching, and I love to travel, and I don't need to sacrifice one for the other. So my new itinerary for life involves teaching in new places so that I can continue to experience new cultures, people, ideas, etc. I'm moving to Europe in September where I'll be teaching in Portugal. Thank you, the book helped me realize that I had more control over my future than I was allowing for."

Ignacio's Story

In Spain, Ignacio Monedero was thirty-six years old and at a crossroads, deciding on his next career move. When he asked me about my writing, I told him that it was a documentation of the success principles I'd studied and used in my life and career and that these tools had worked very effectively for me and for many others.

I gave him a draft of the first two chapters and soon received the following email from him: "In these last few years, I've had a remote wish which struck me as a foolish fancy, but now that I've read the first part of your book, I look at it as something achievable: why not? You have given me the push that I need to start fighting for it with strength because now, I find it possible."

He agreed to apply the ideas from the book to help him to fulfill his dream. He became increasingly excited as he began to get results. About mid-way through the book Ignacio said, "Up to this point in my life, I've been holding back from going after my dreams because of a fear of failure. (Does that sound familiar to you, too?) It's as though I were in the locker room at a track meet, dressed, my track shoes on, ready to compete, but afraid to go out on the track. Since I've been reading your book I feel that now I'm out on the track, at the starting line."

As the months went by Ignacio set goals, experienced setbacks, persevered and finally realized the first important result of his definite major purpose.

Other Successes

An energetic and smiling Bethel greeted me at the post office with an enthusiastic hug. She had left the closeness and security of her family and friends in the small town where she grew up, and moved to Santa Fe. In spite of her smiles, Bethel was nursing a broken heart from a serious relationship and was back home to regain her focus in the warmth of her family. However, her parents were divorcing and she realized that she needed to make some positive changes and improvements in her life.

What a great summer that turned to be! Bethel agreed to read my manuscript one chapter a week and report her progress to me. Through tears and frustrations she worked hard on setting and achieving meaningful goals and identifying her purpose in life. In her words, "I wanted to work on some behaviors I didn't like and Byron's manuscript was one of the tools the universe gave me during that trying time in my life. I am now happily married to the man of my dreams. Every day I work on becoming a better wife, friend, sister, and daughter—but it was that one summer that really helped mold how I am today."

Jenny de la Casa, age twenty-five, is an administrative assistant in a government agency in Canada. "The book has started me thinking about my current situation (and what I like about it). There are a lot of things for me to do. I have tons of ideas of what I want to do (like own my own business) but I'm a big procrastinator. The book has given me the pieces of the puzzle to help me find out where I want to go."

These examples tell you what exciting changes are taking place in these people's lives! They are each creating their own dreams by courageously taking control of their lives and following a few tested principals from this book. You can too!

You can see why I'm excited.

Many times an author's intentions and the reader's understanding are different. I know what my intentions were; let's see how your understanding matches that intention by making a checklist of where we are before we start on the next phase.

1. We recognize that there is the possibility of an even more rewarding life and we're able to create it for ourselves.

2. We have a major purpose.

3. We've come to recognize the power and importance of thought.

4. We have a powerful vision of the "person I want to be."

5. We have set goals for the important areas of our lives.

6. We use treasure mapping and affirmations to help us achieve our goals.

7. We have an understanding of our barriers and distractions and developed strategies for overcoming them.

8. We've developed the habit of keeping a journal and use notes of appreciation.

9. We recognize the value and importance of people.

10. We clearly understand our own and others' motivations.

11. We know the value of being self-directed and managing ourselves.

The next and most important step in the process is for you to create your own action program. Think of each of the above items on your checklist as tools to assist you with the task of building your ideal life.

Pursuing a purpose is not the same as striving for a goal, with quantifiable dimensions. Our purpose will always be expanding.

We will never be self-actualizing all the time, nor will we attain perfection, which is really good news. We would not want to lose our humanity. Mythologist Joseph Campbell said, "Perfection is not lovable, and the traits that make us all human are our imperfections."

For those times when we do attain our ideal, what does it look like? My description would be the following:

- One feels a sense of satisfaction and contentment.

- One responds to setbacks as challenges, and treats them as problems to be solved, as in a game.

- One feels at cause, in control.

- Things seem orderly, appropriate and relevant.

- One feels blessed and worthy.

- One has a sense of mission with significant work to do.

- One feels integrated, whole, at home with oneself.

- One feels valuable, worthwhile, and useful, and his or her actions are perceived as having an impact on others and making a difference in the world.

- One feels as though they are complete, as though nothing is missing.

- One perceives himself or herself as large, consequential, and important.

- One is perceived to be genuine, and in fact, *is* genuine.

- One keeps his or her promises. They do what they say and say what they do. They can be counted on. They are not discordant. They walk their talk.

- Most of all, one feels totally alive, challenged and excited.

Good luck! You now have your bag of tools and book of rules for creating *A Life Worth Living*. Your success is important to me. Let me know how you're doing.

Acknowledgements

I am a product of all the forces that have influenced me. Many authors have shaped my thinking and ideas. Clients and course participants, employees, and associates have all touched my life. I appreciate all their input and help.

Patricia, my wife, best friend, and partner has been my most ardent supporter and thankfully, my most honest critic. She has not allowed me to compromise any of the issues relating to accuracy and excellence. Thank you to Michelle and Ana, my daughters, for providing me with the inspiration of love and the motivation to create a worthwhile life for all of us.

With honest, sincere, appreciation to L. G. (Boo) Bue, my mentor and friend, whose faith sustained me and who held me to the highest possible standard of excellence.

To my friends Bob James, Jay Westrom, Eddie Snow, Lee Straughan, Kevin Crone, and all of the great people in the Dale Carnegie organization worldwide, who have taught me, inspired me, and shared the love of helping people grow.

Special thanks to that group of people who took the time to read the manuscript and give me their honest feedback:

Scott Davis, David Bond, Eric Merk, Danita Wampole, Tony Monaghan, Gwen Crowell, Mike Crowell, Elizabeth Apt, Jenny de la Casa, Bethel Honan, James Shull, Chad Atwood, Aprile Winterstein, Margaret Burgin, Ignacio Monedero, Jayme Westrom, Priscilla MacPherson, Richard Thompson, Mike Schacher, Melissa Schacher, Chuck Iverson, Mike and Anita Sheehan, Henrietta Tseng, Jude Theibert, Adella MacDonald, and Ida Egli.

LaVergne, TN USA
11 September 2009

157628LV00002B/2/P

9 781604 942804